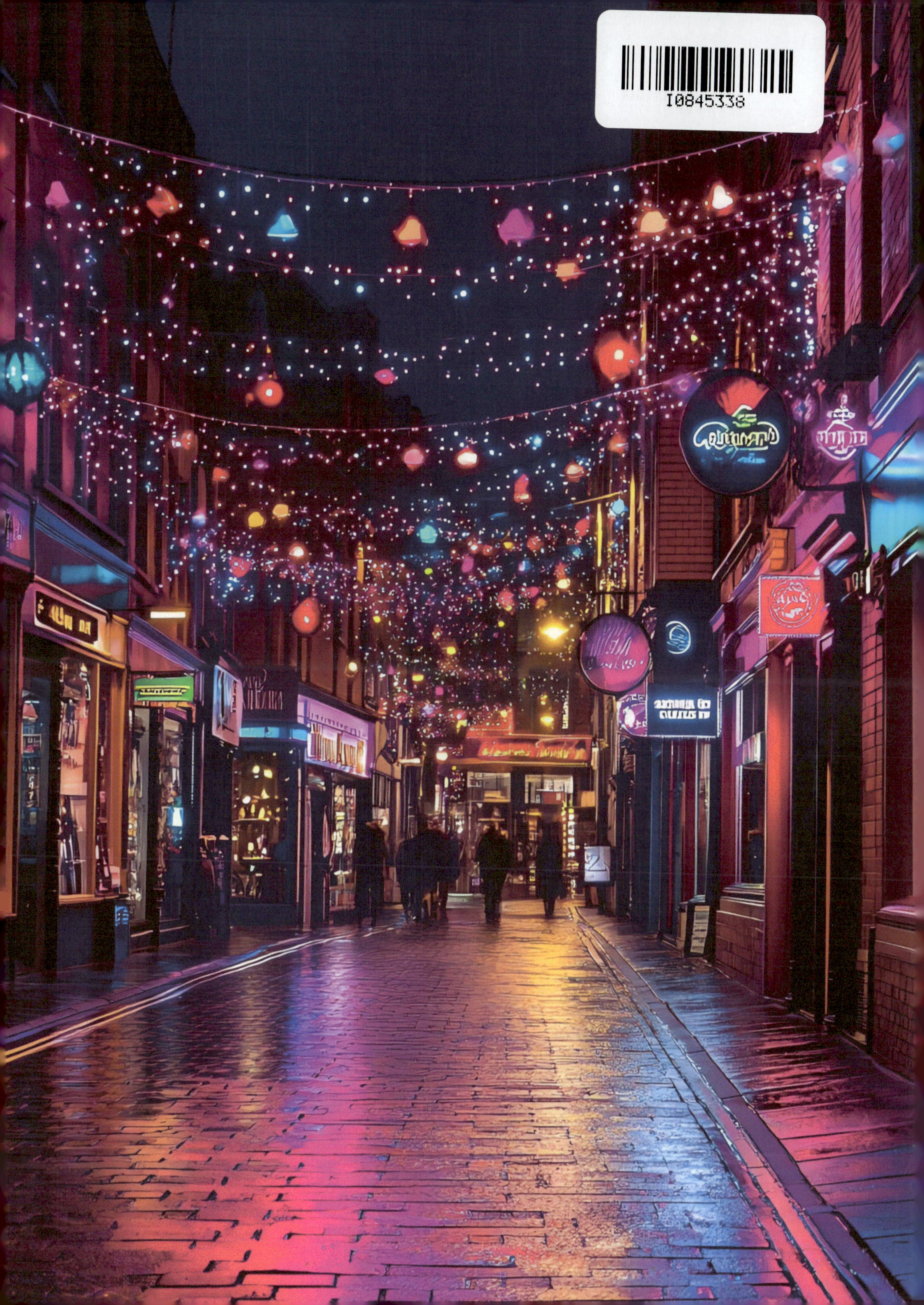

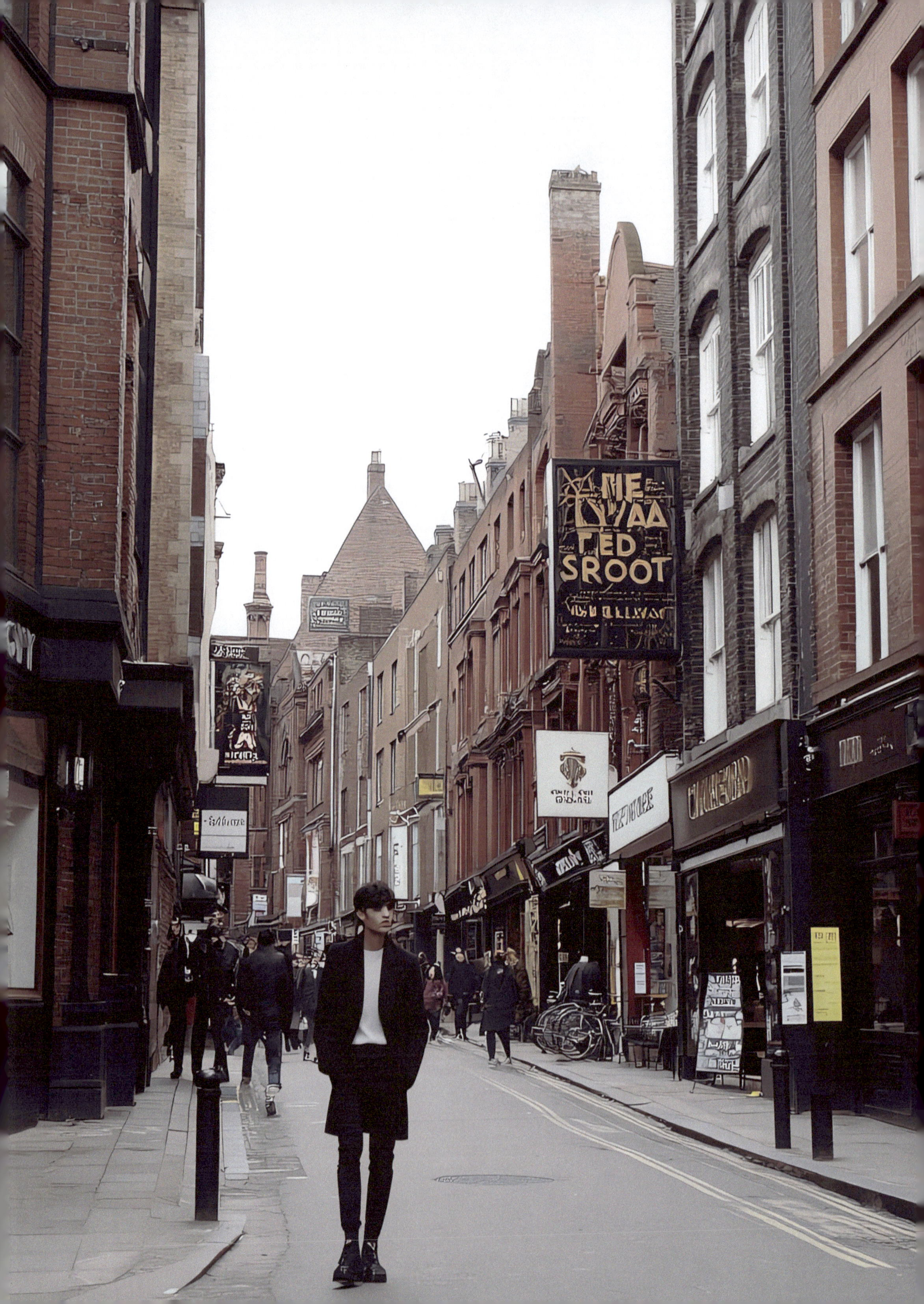
THE
RED
SROOT

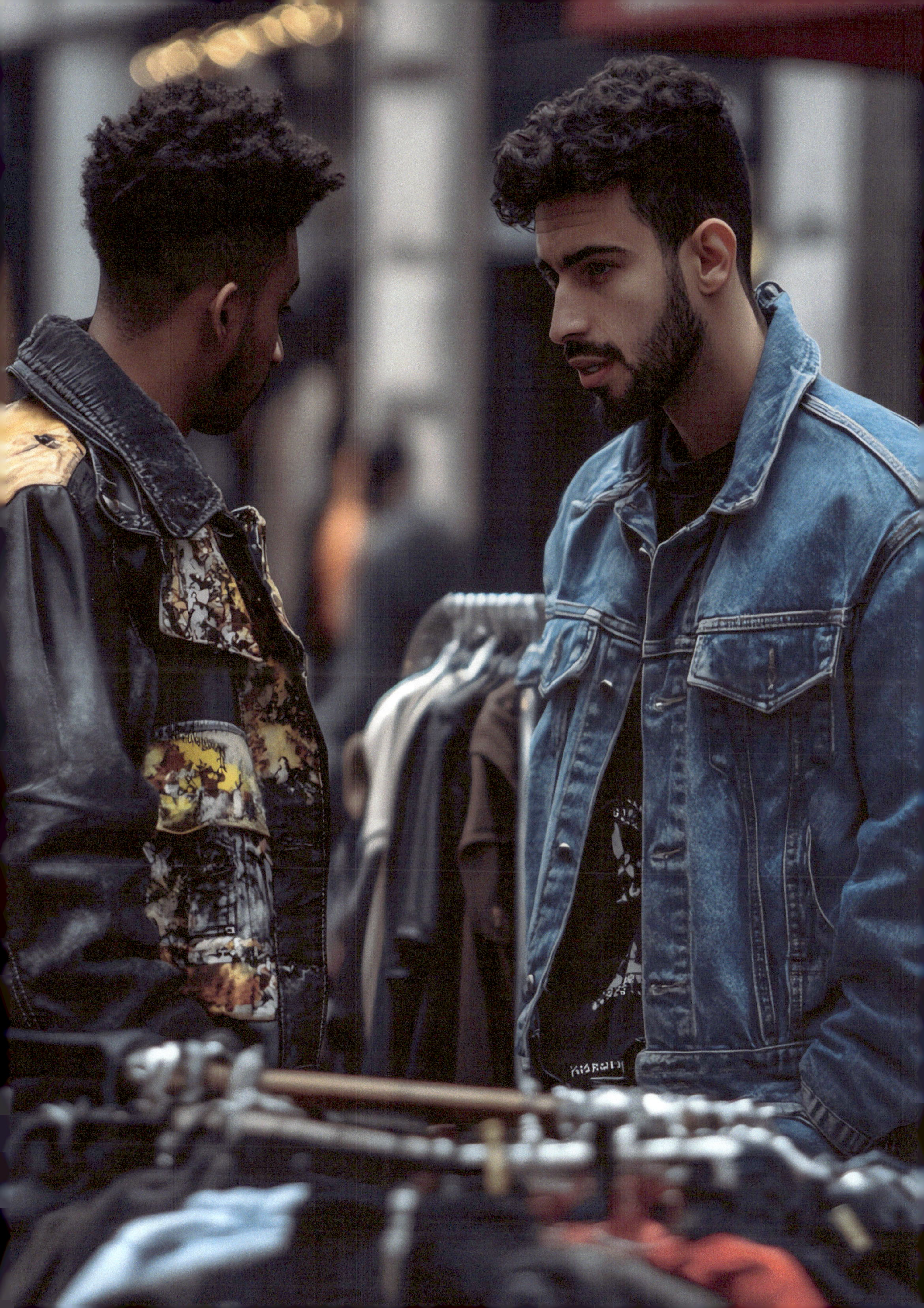

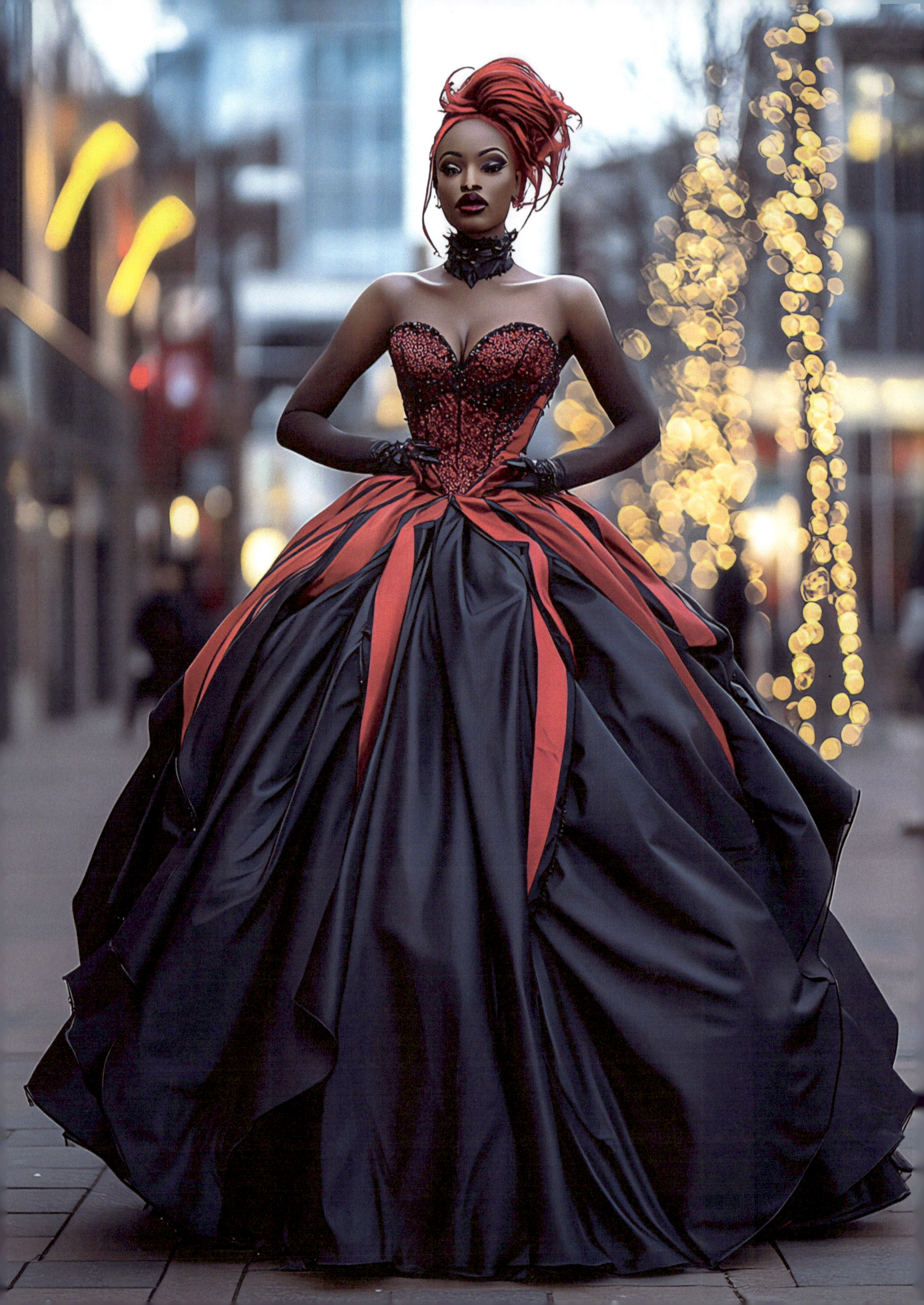

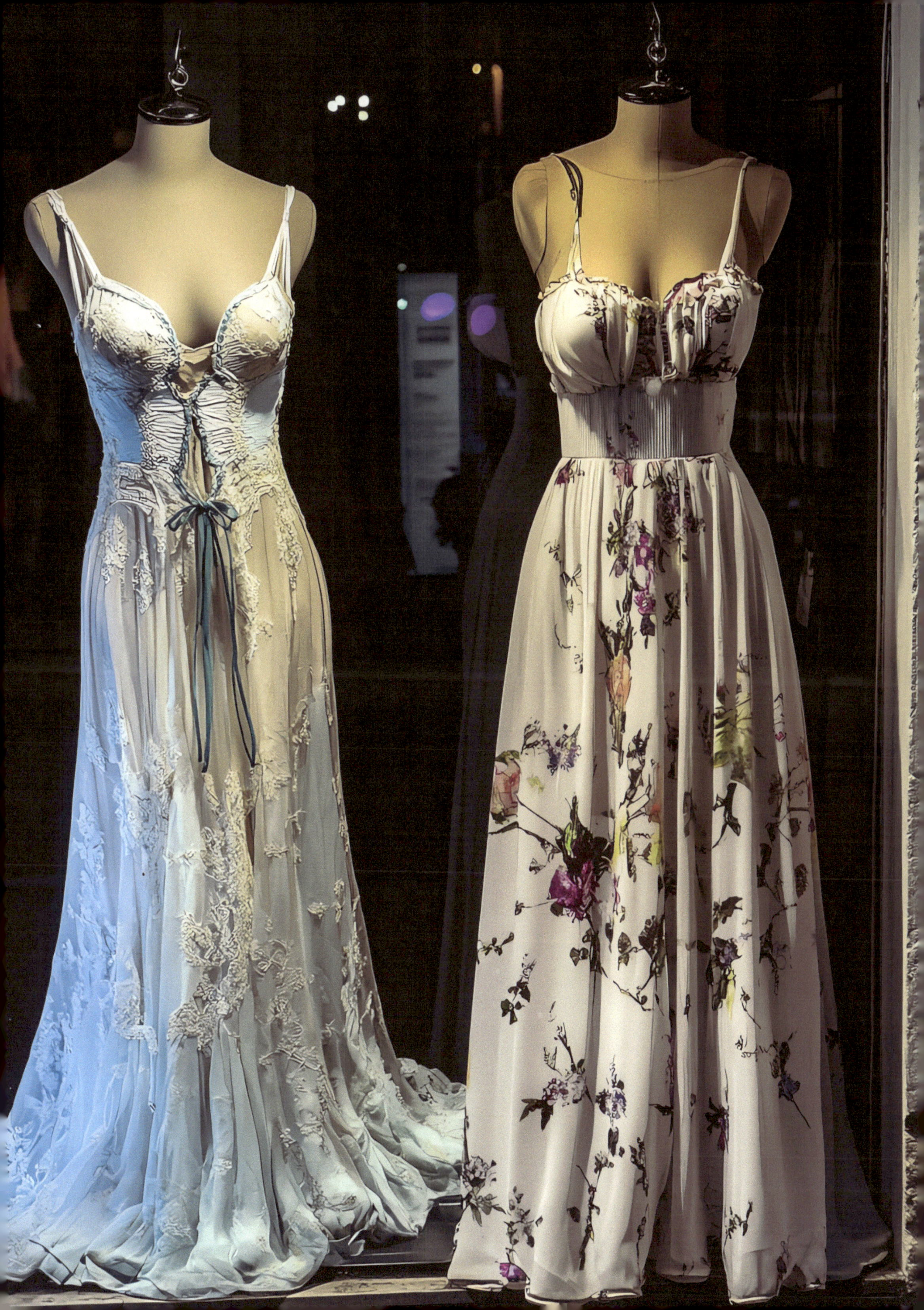

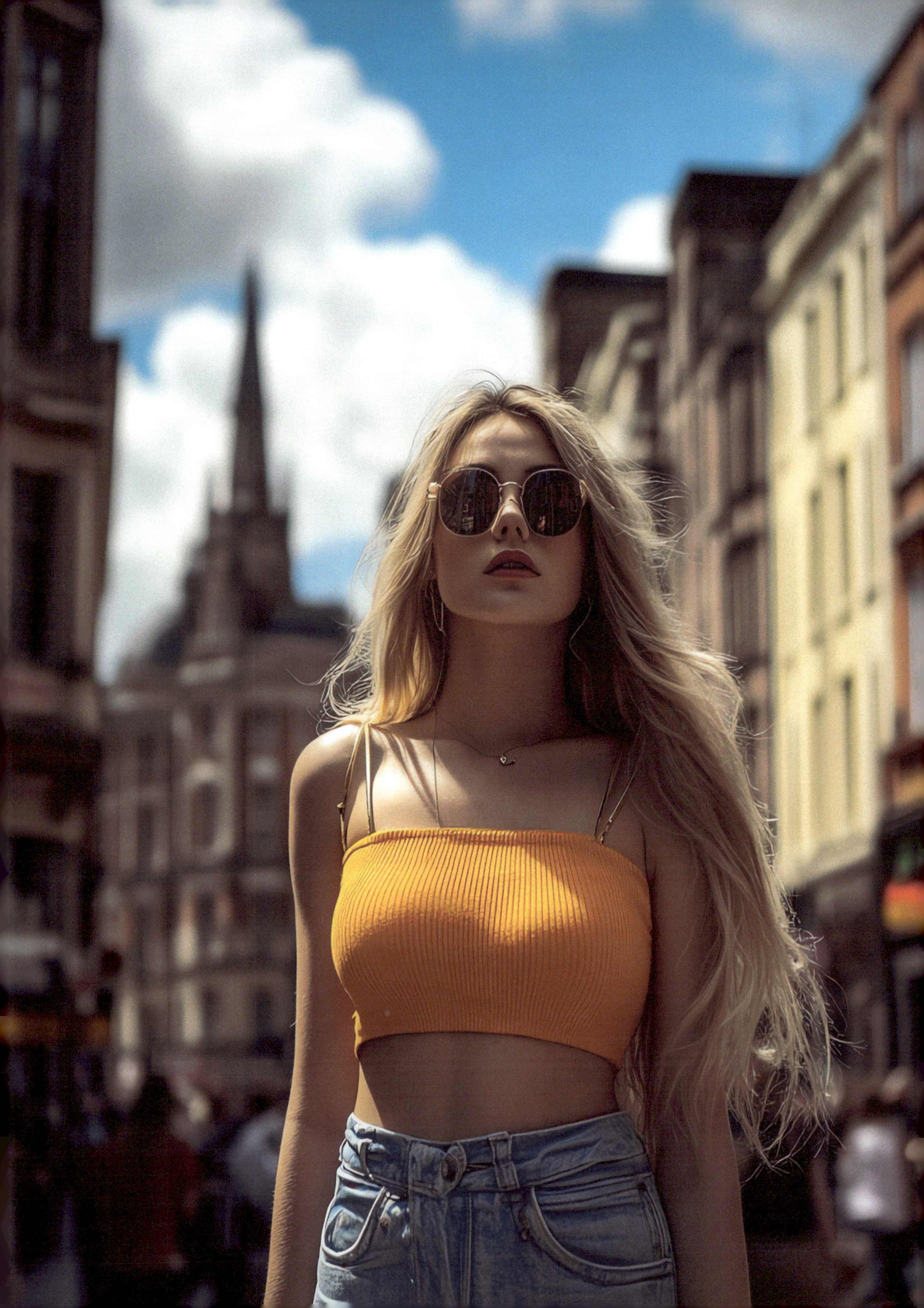

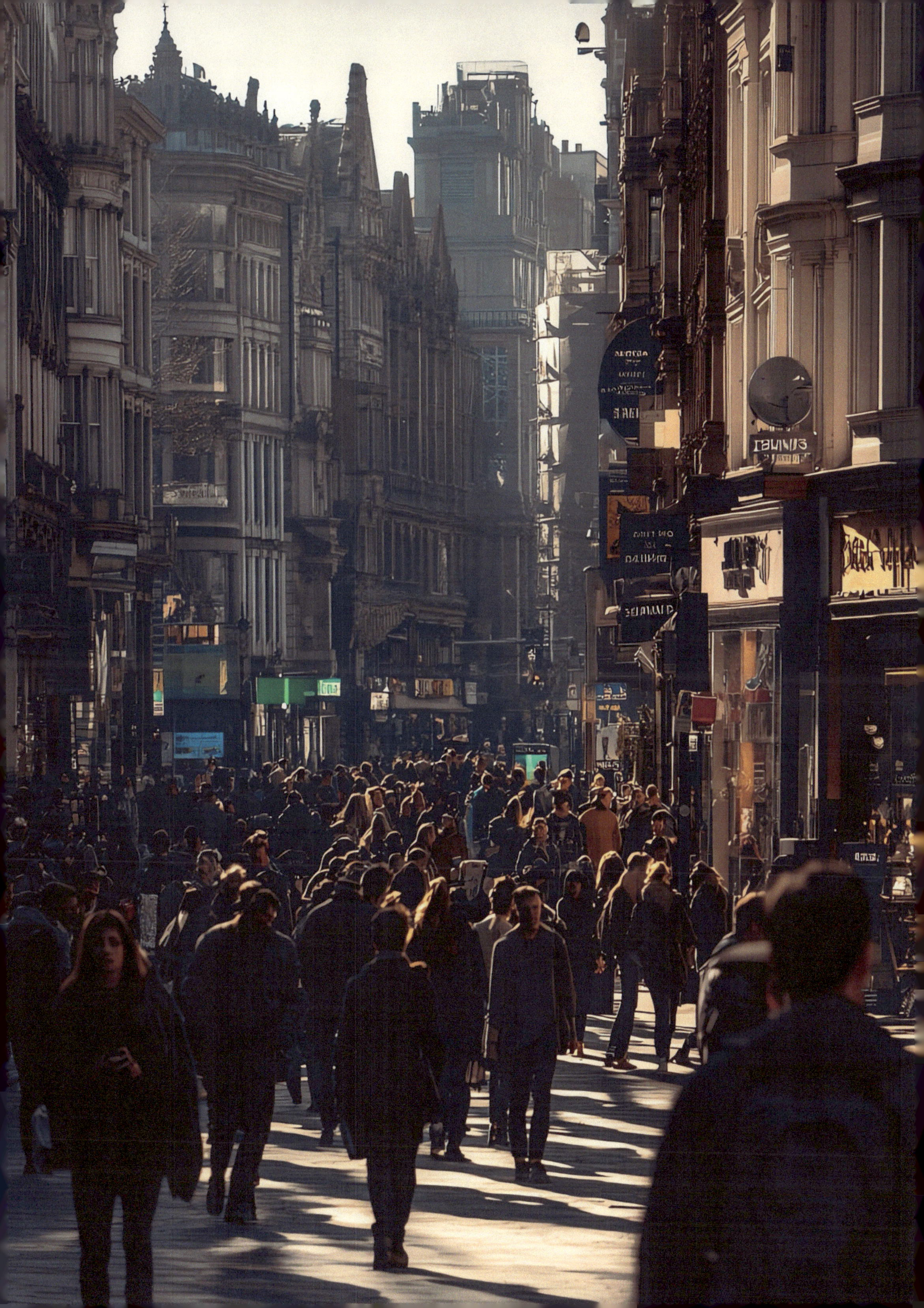

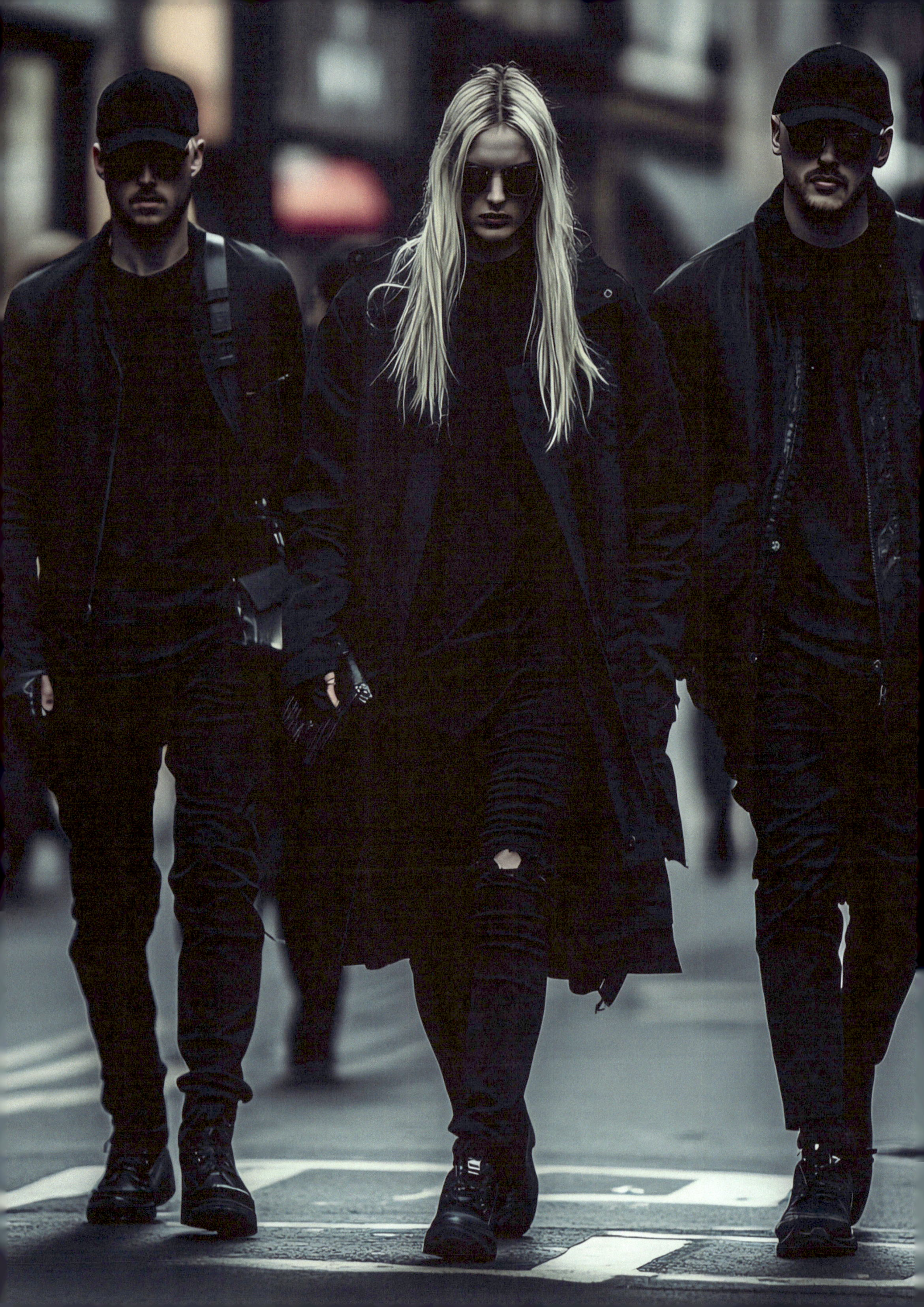

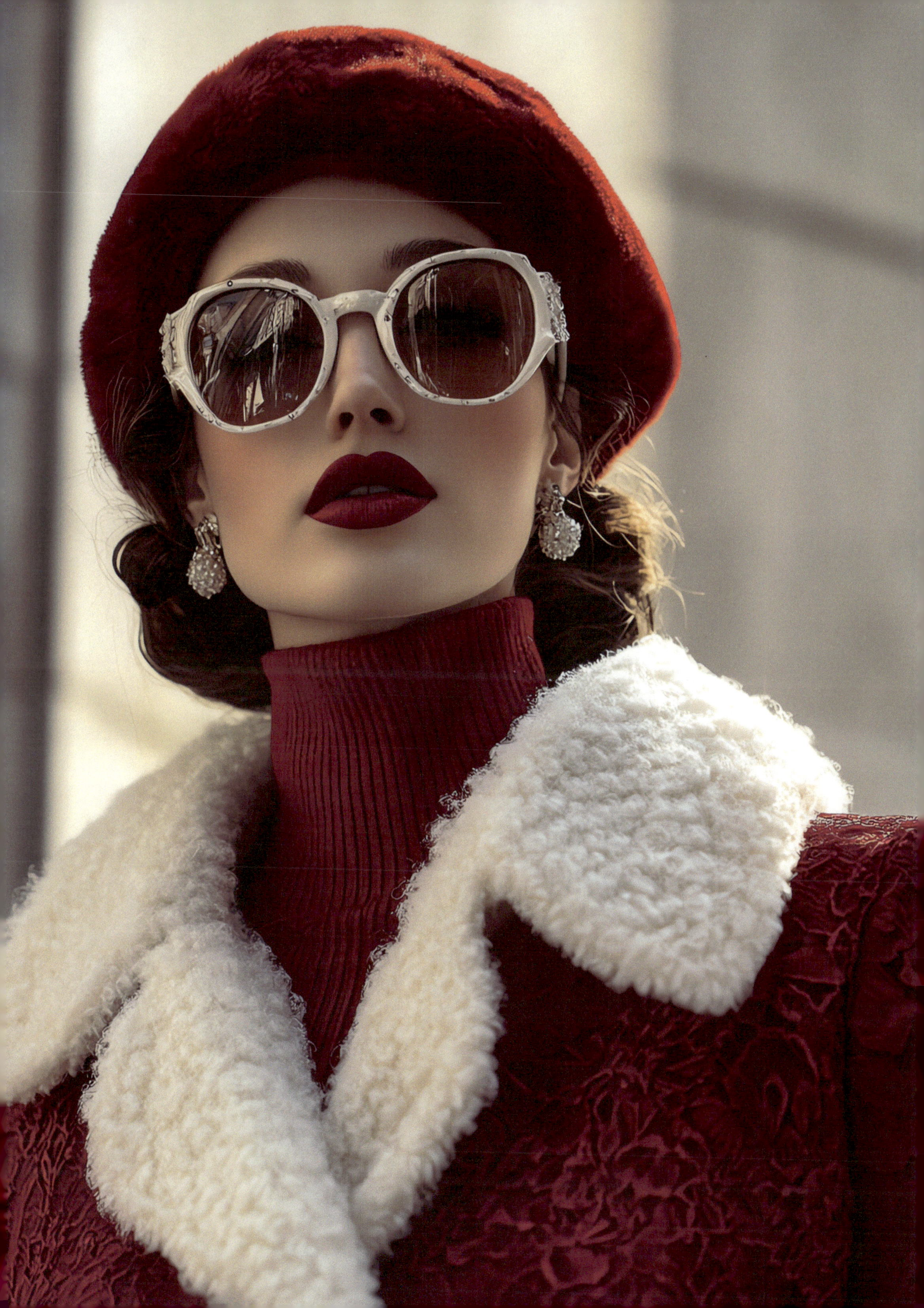

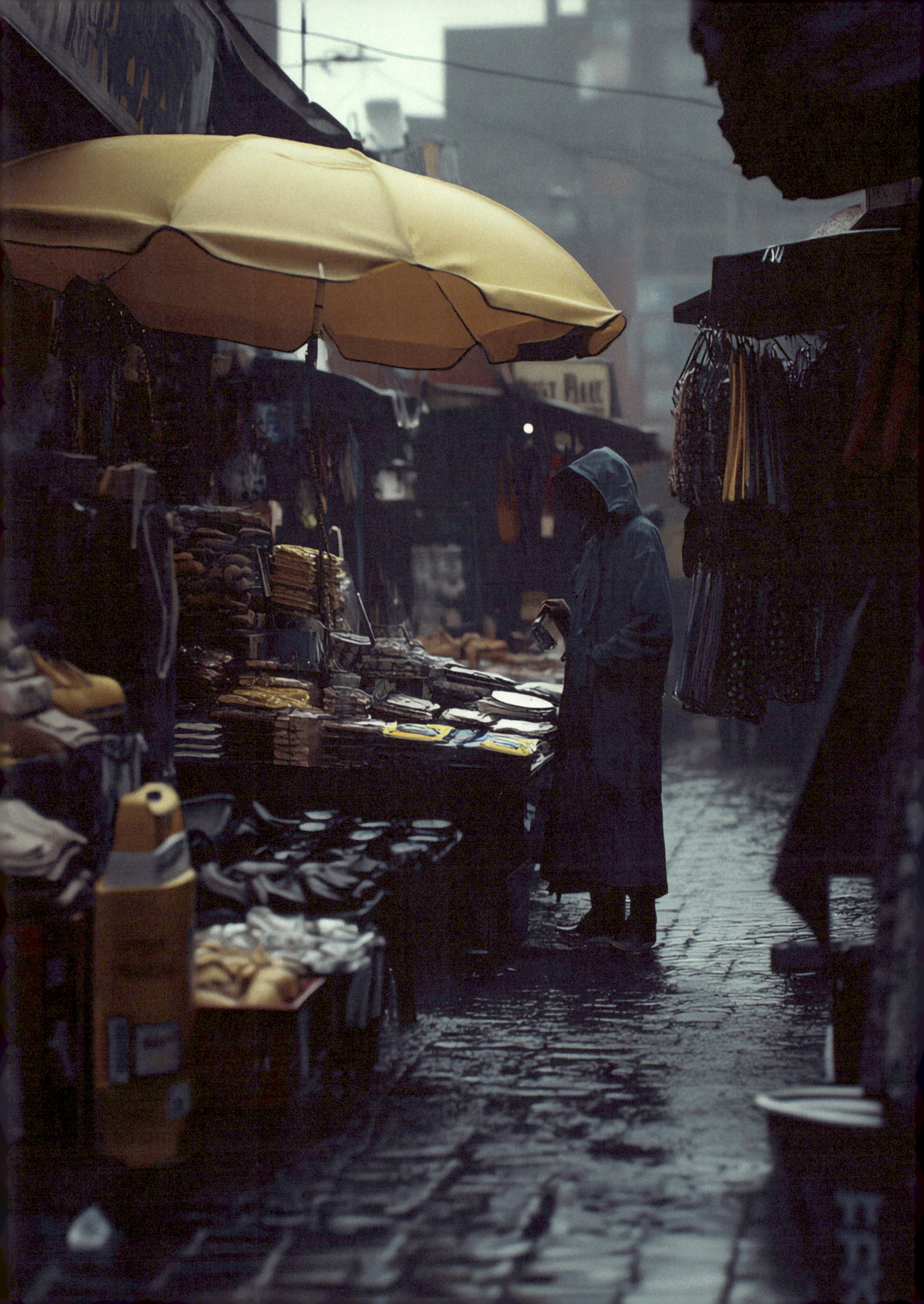

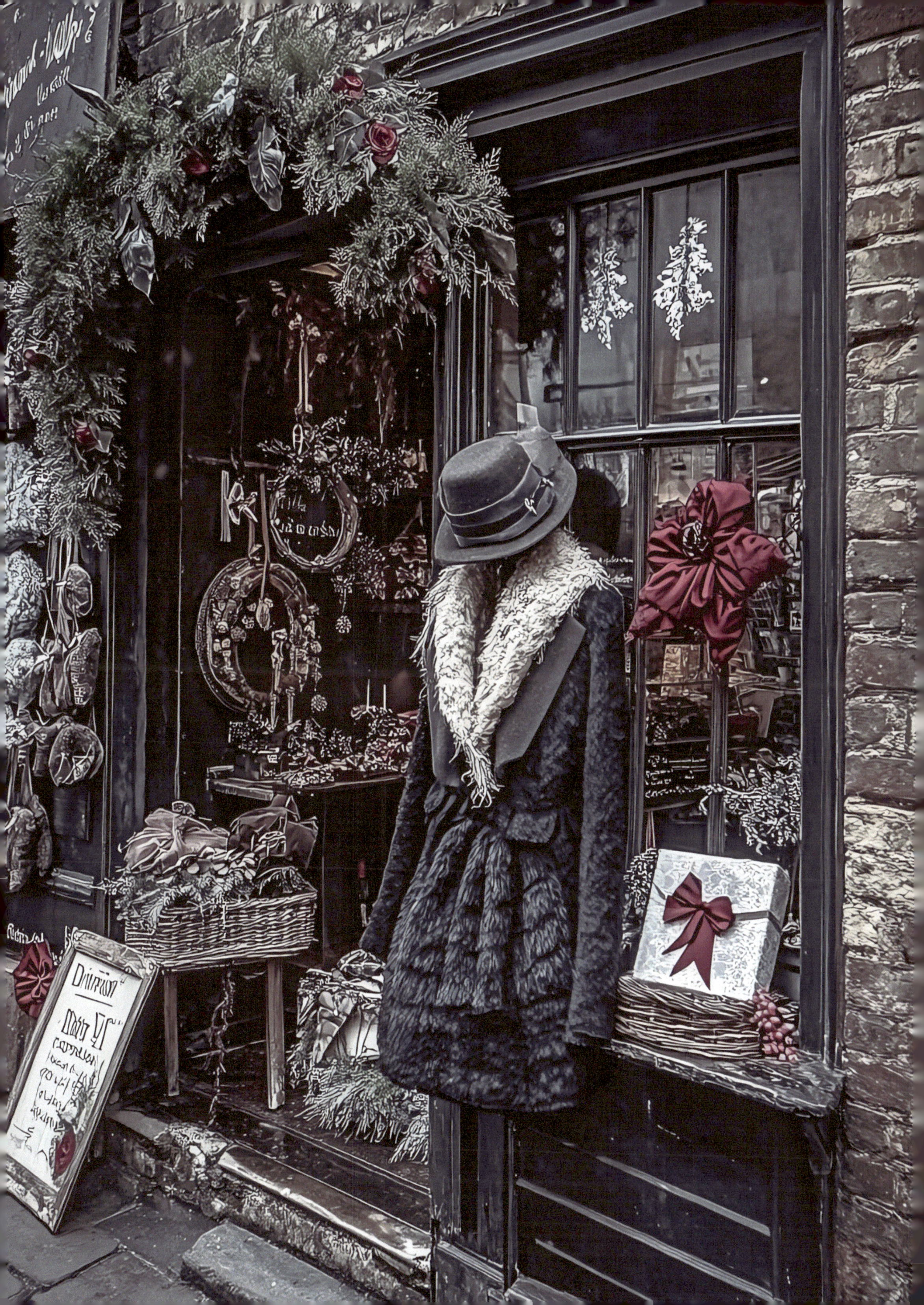

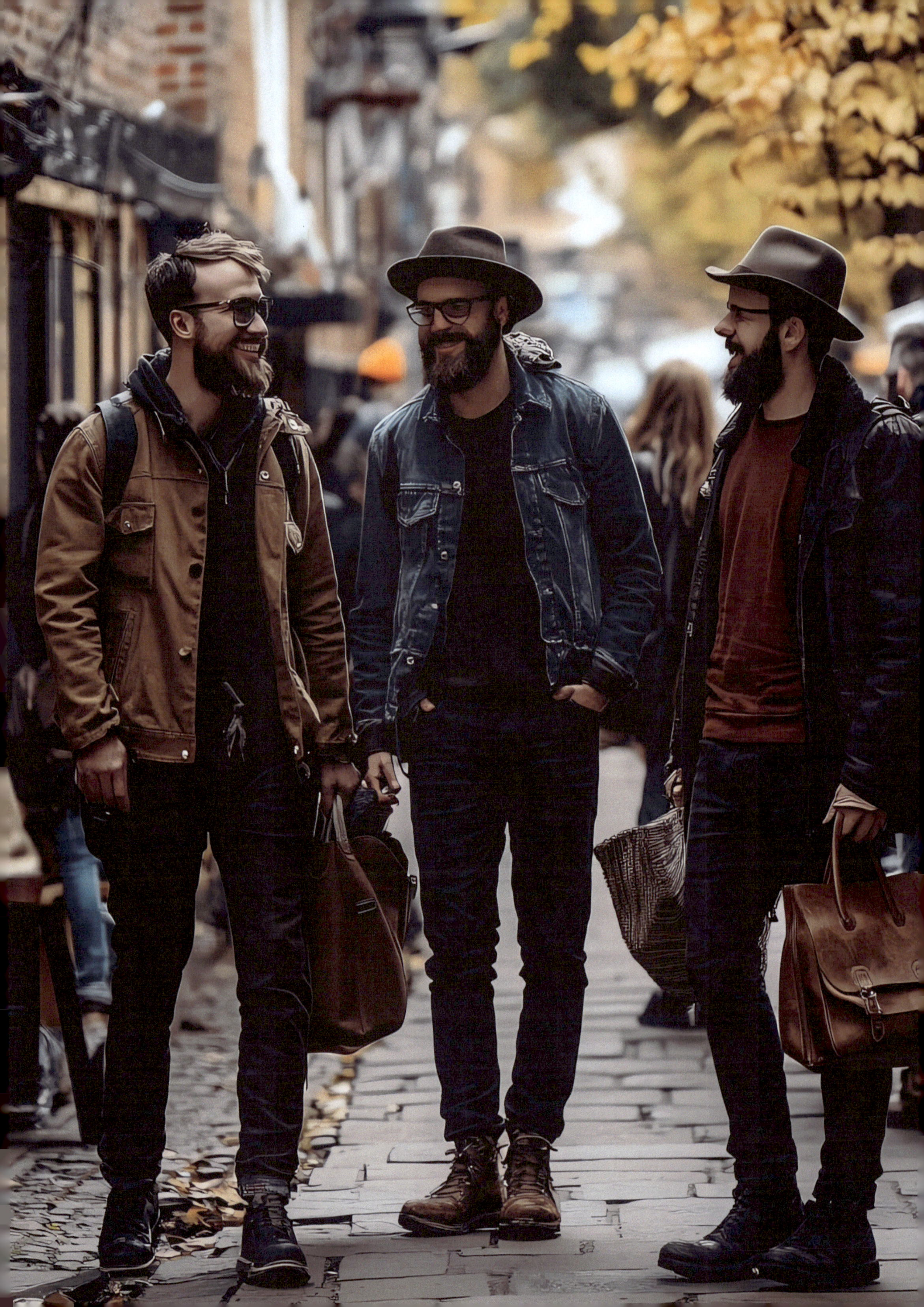

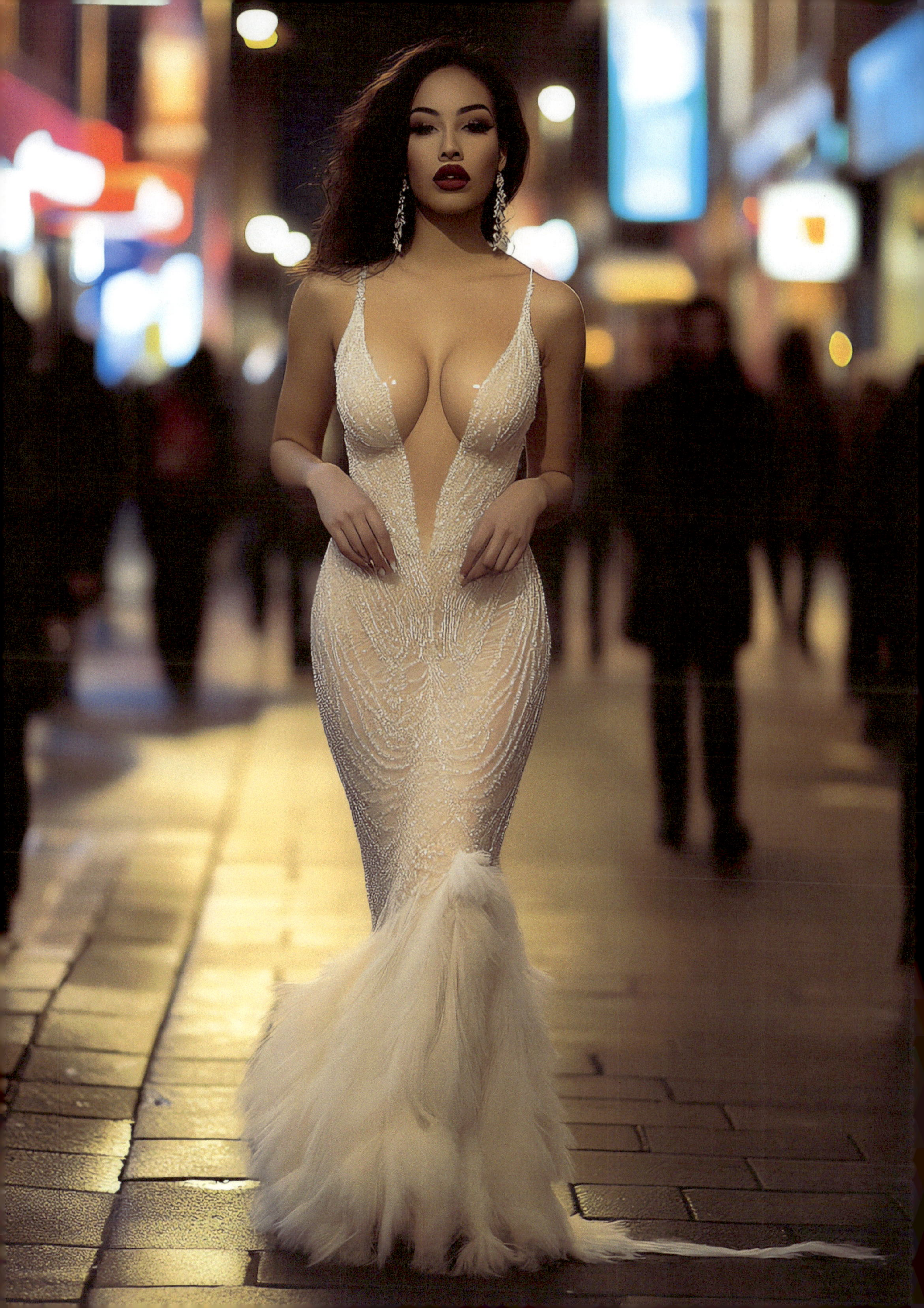

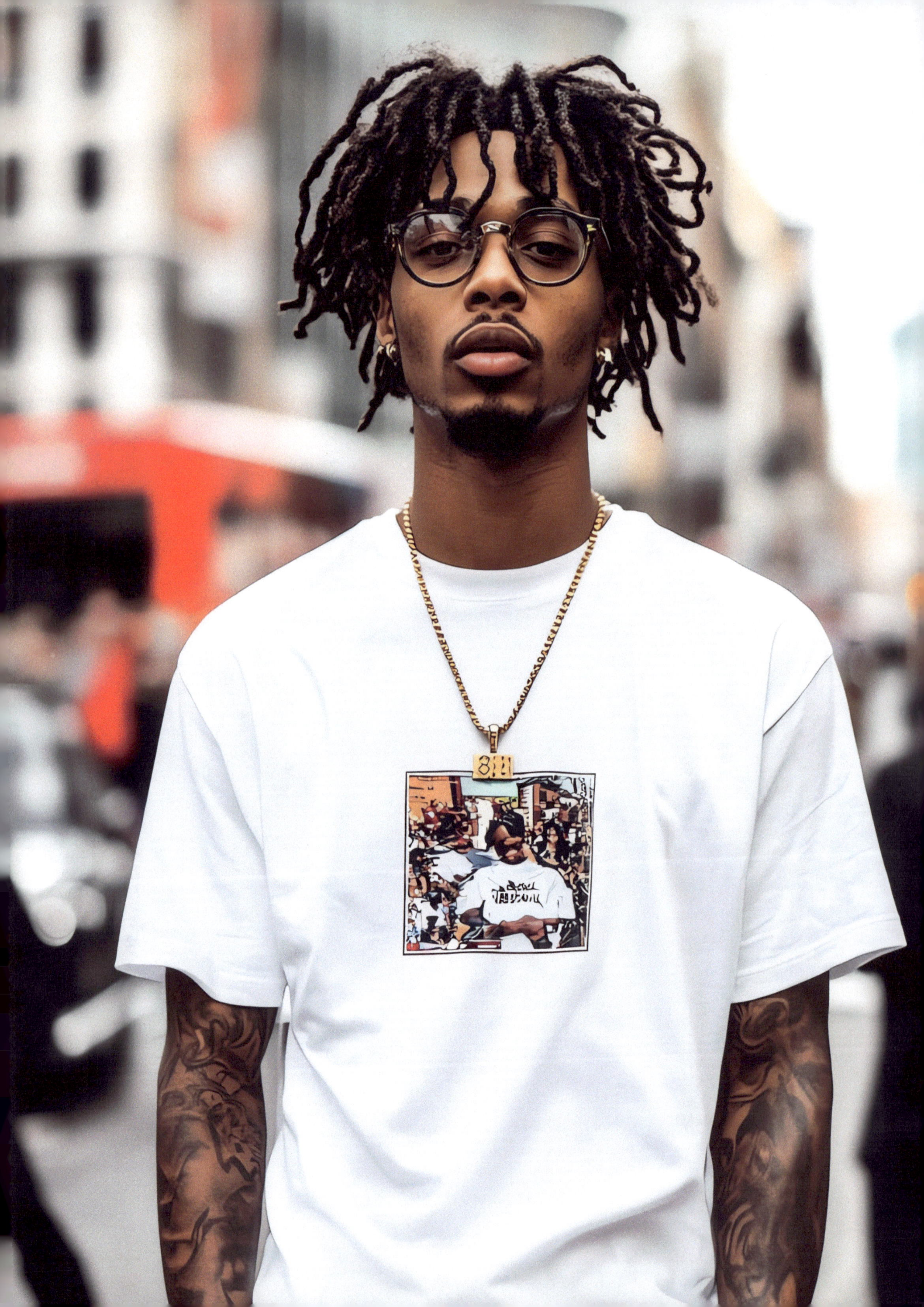

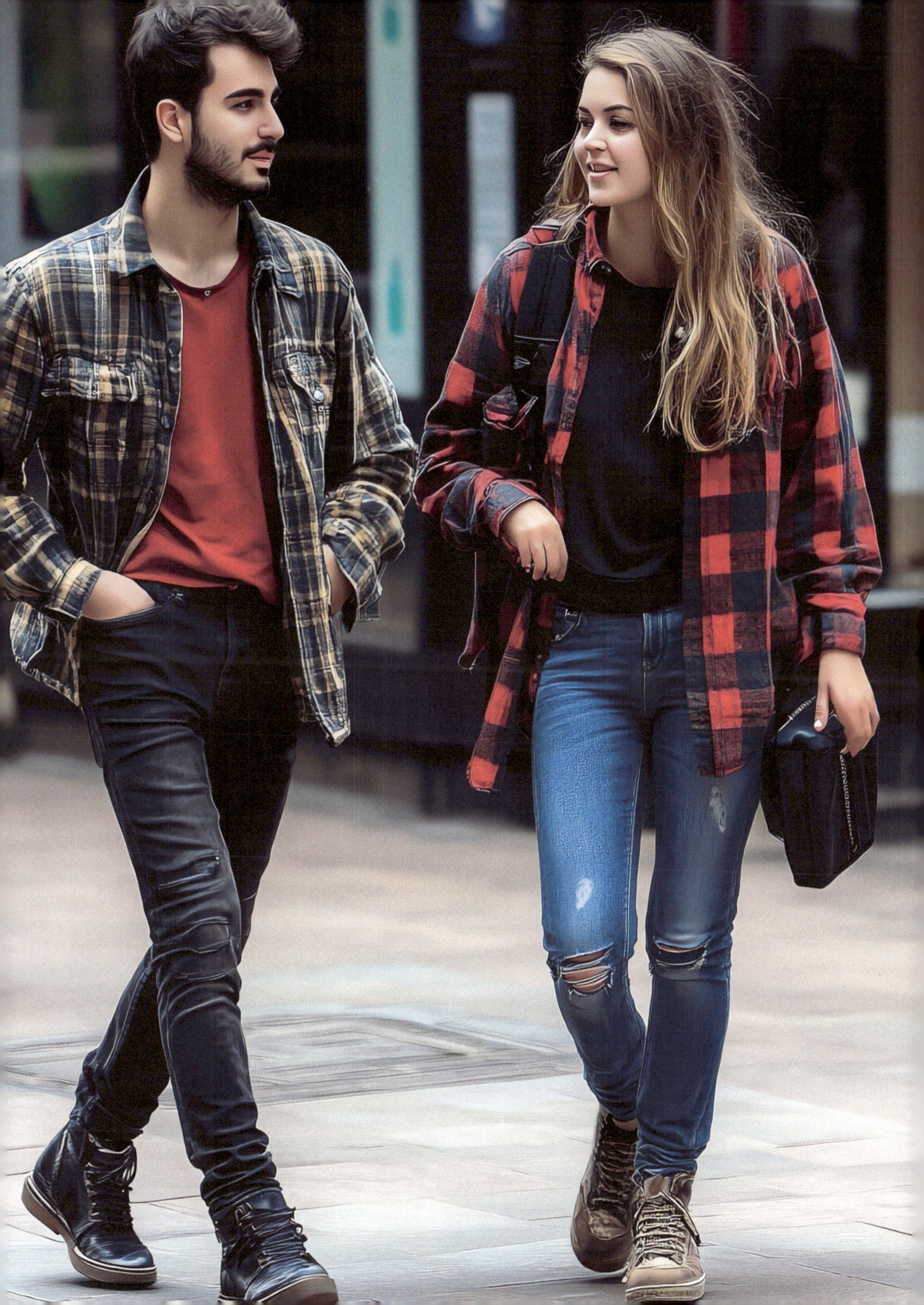

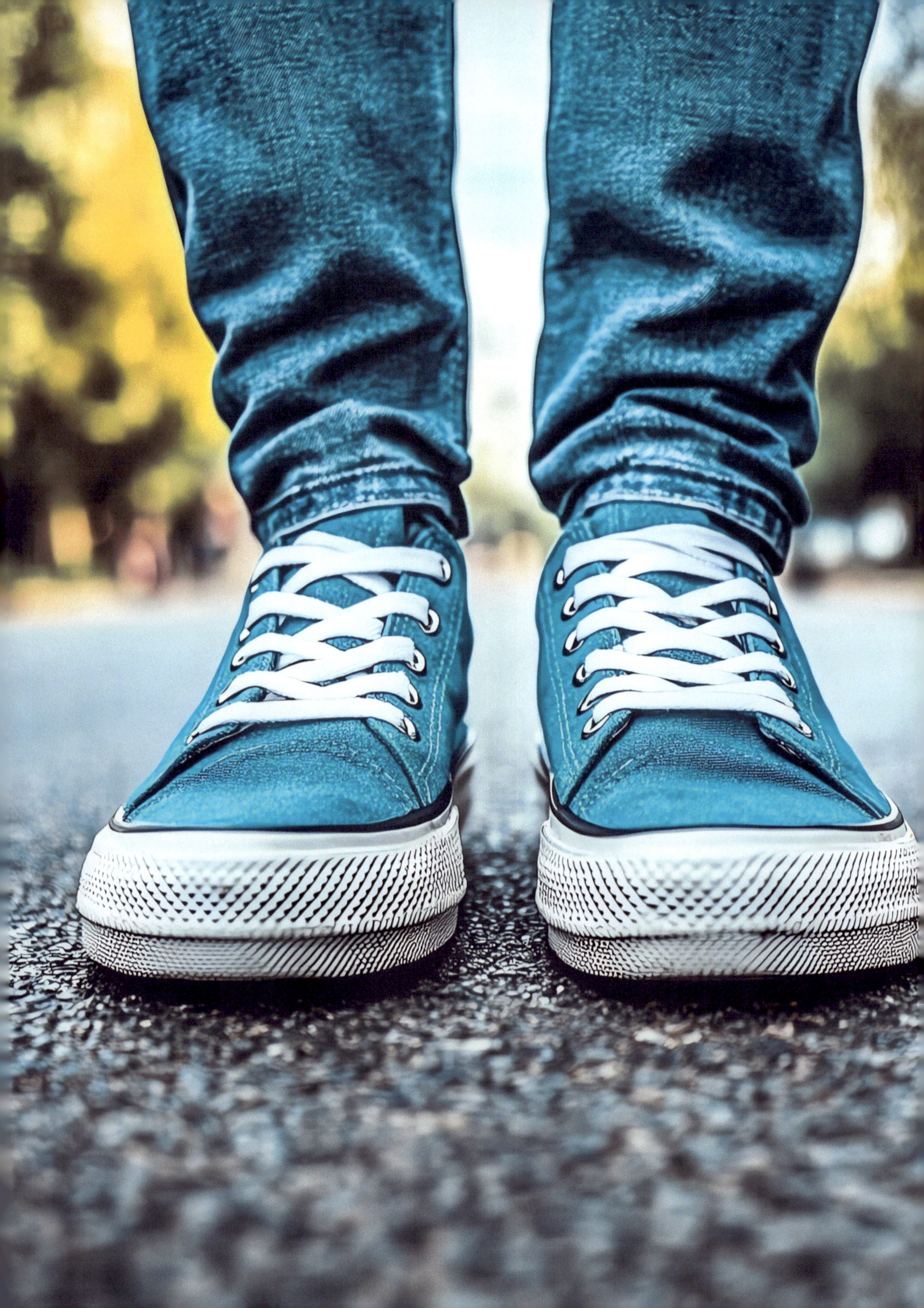

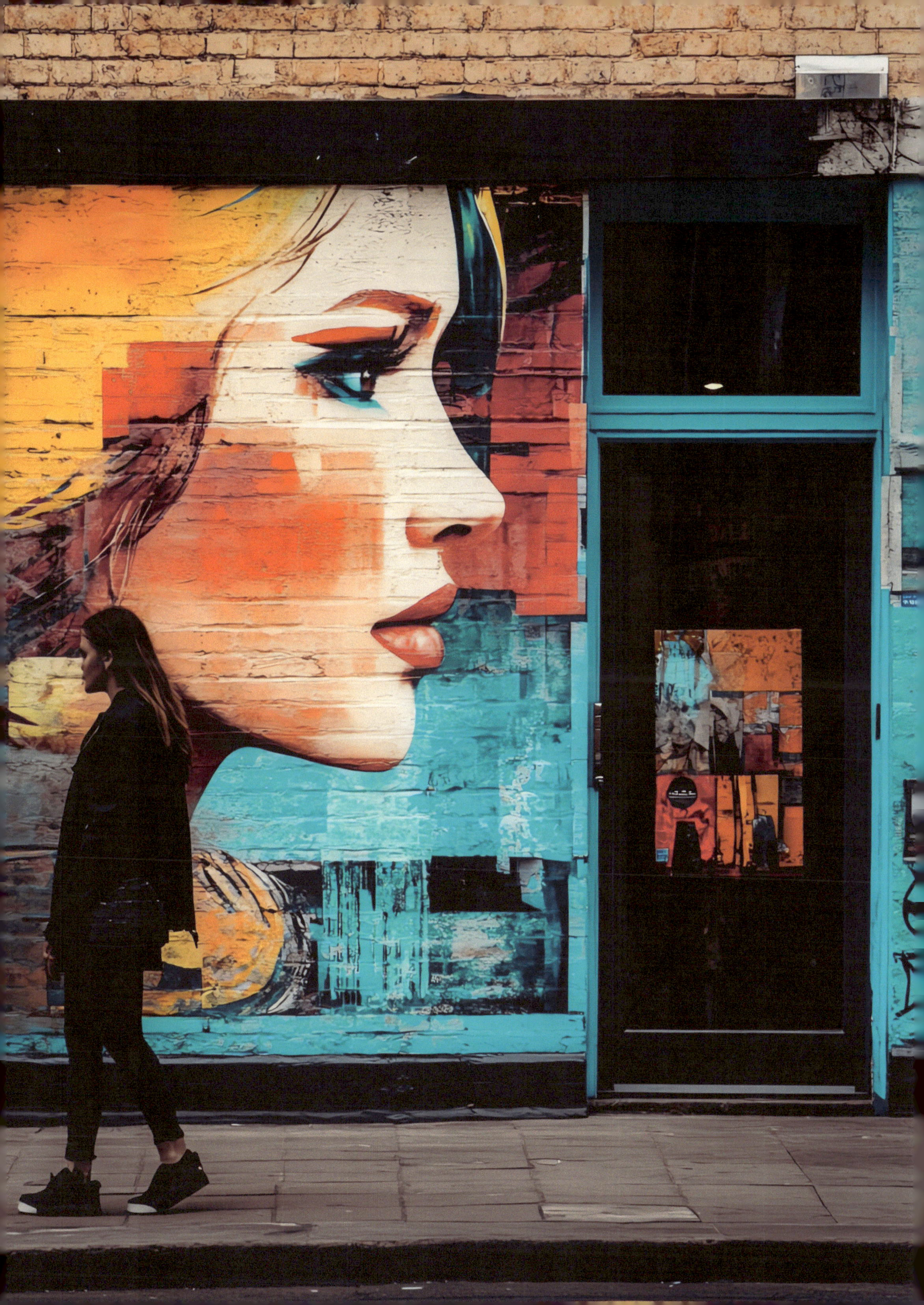

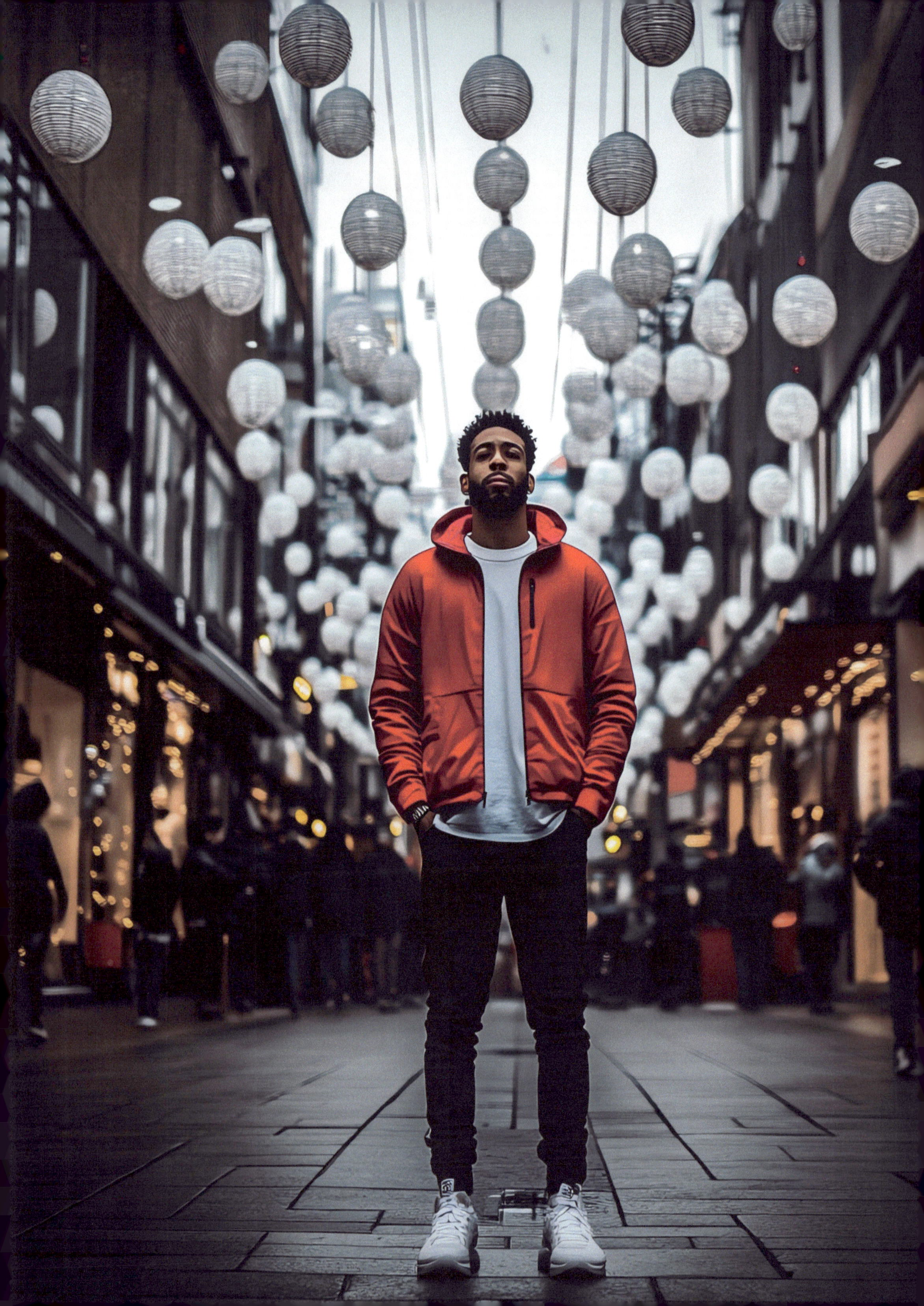

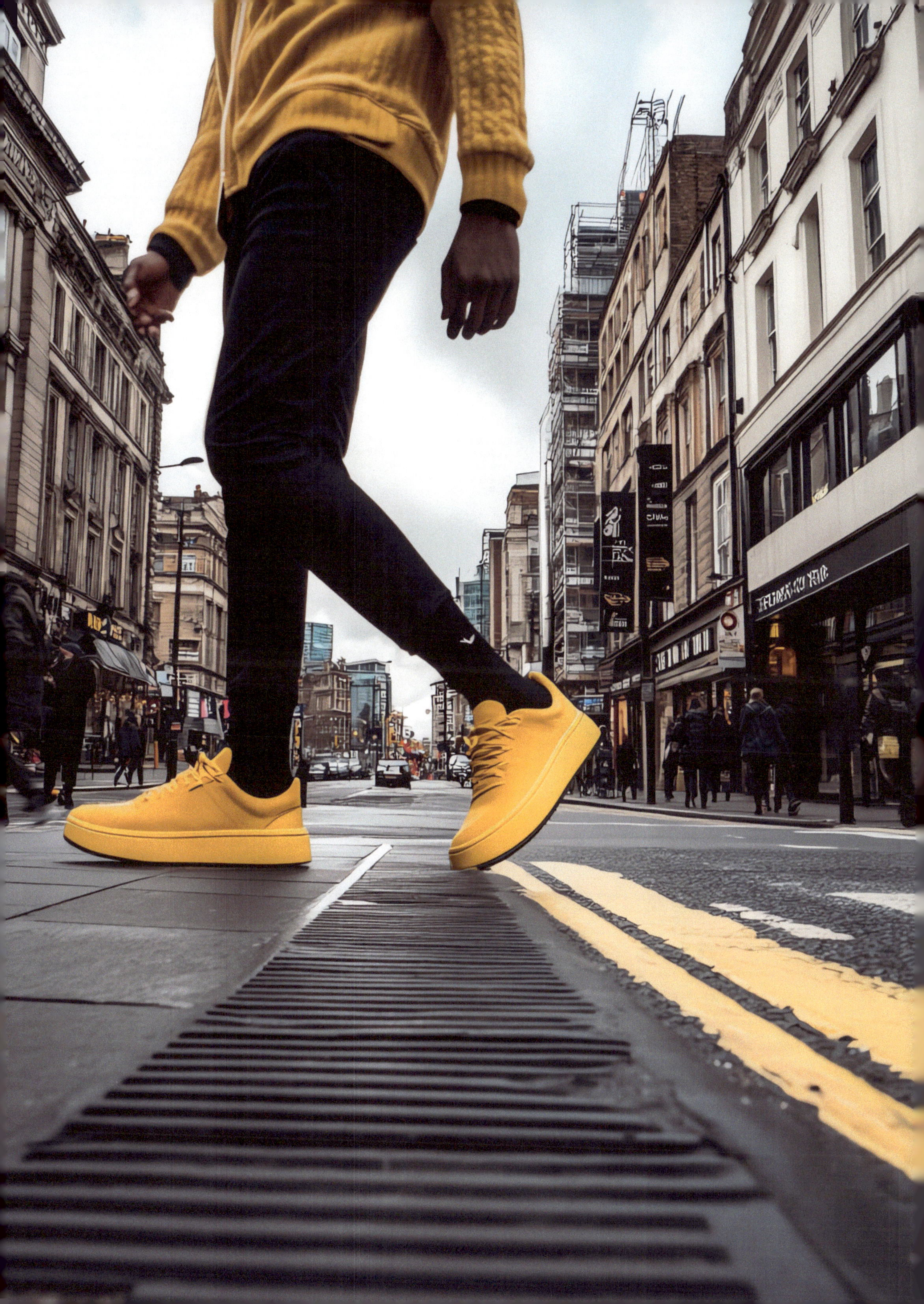

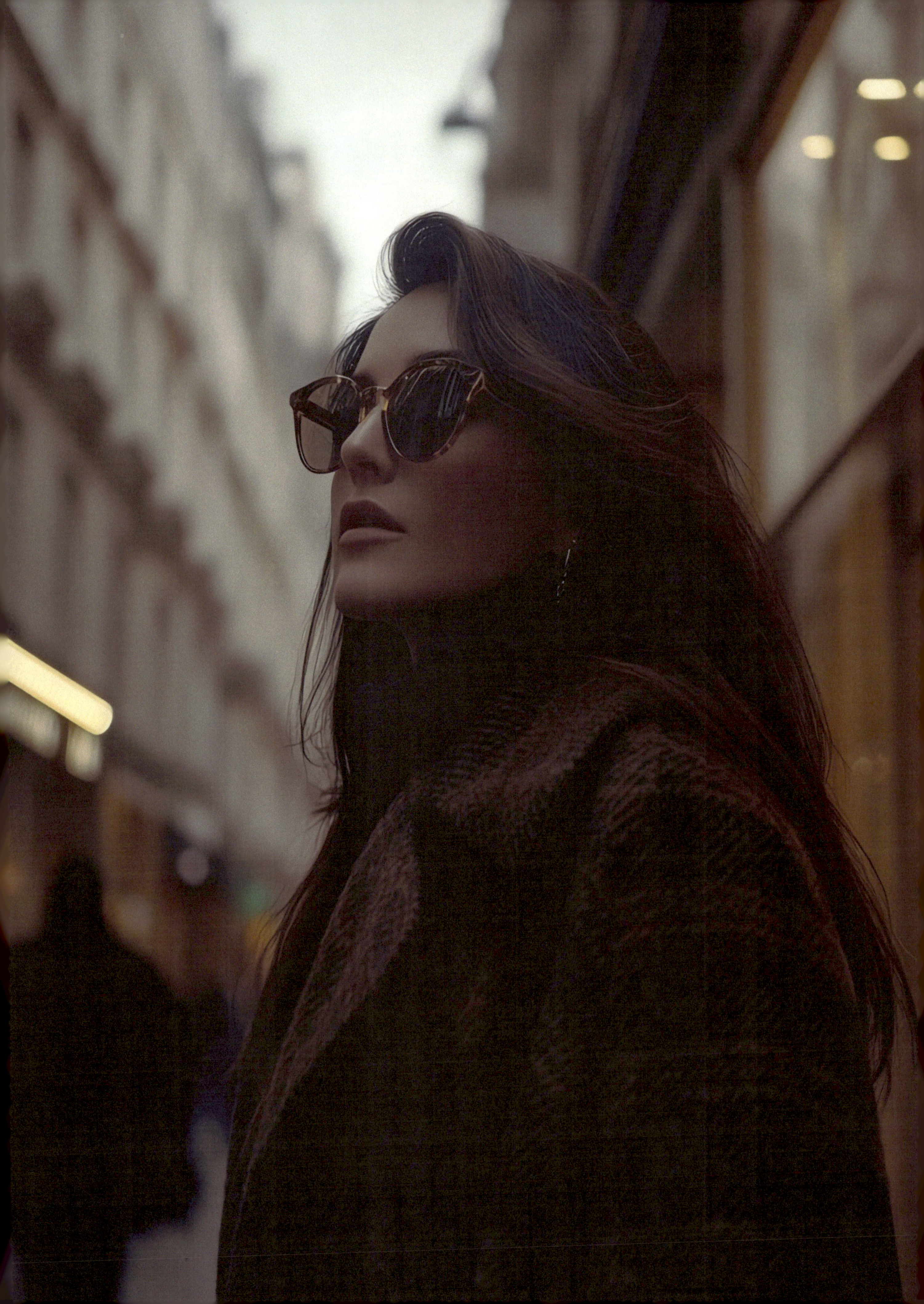

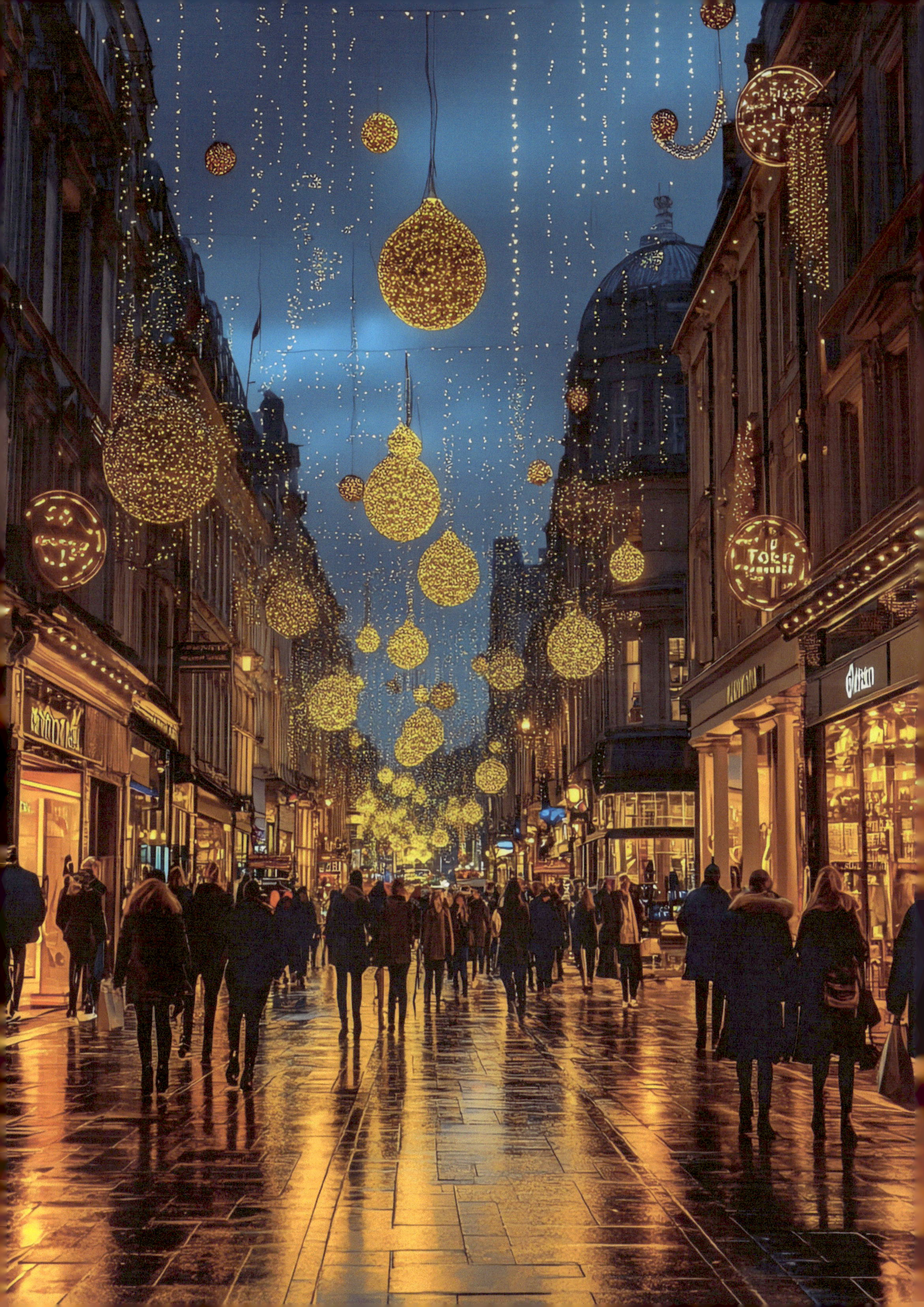

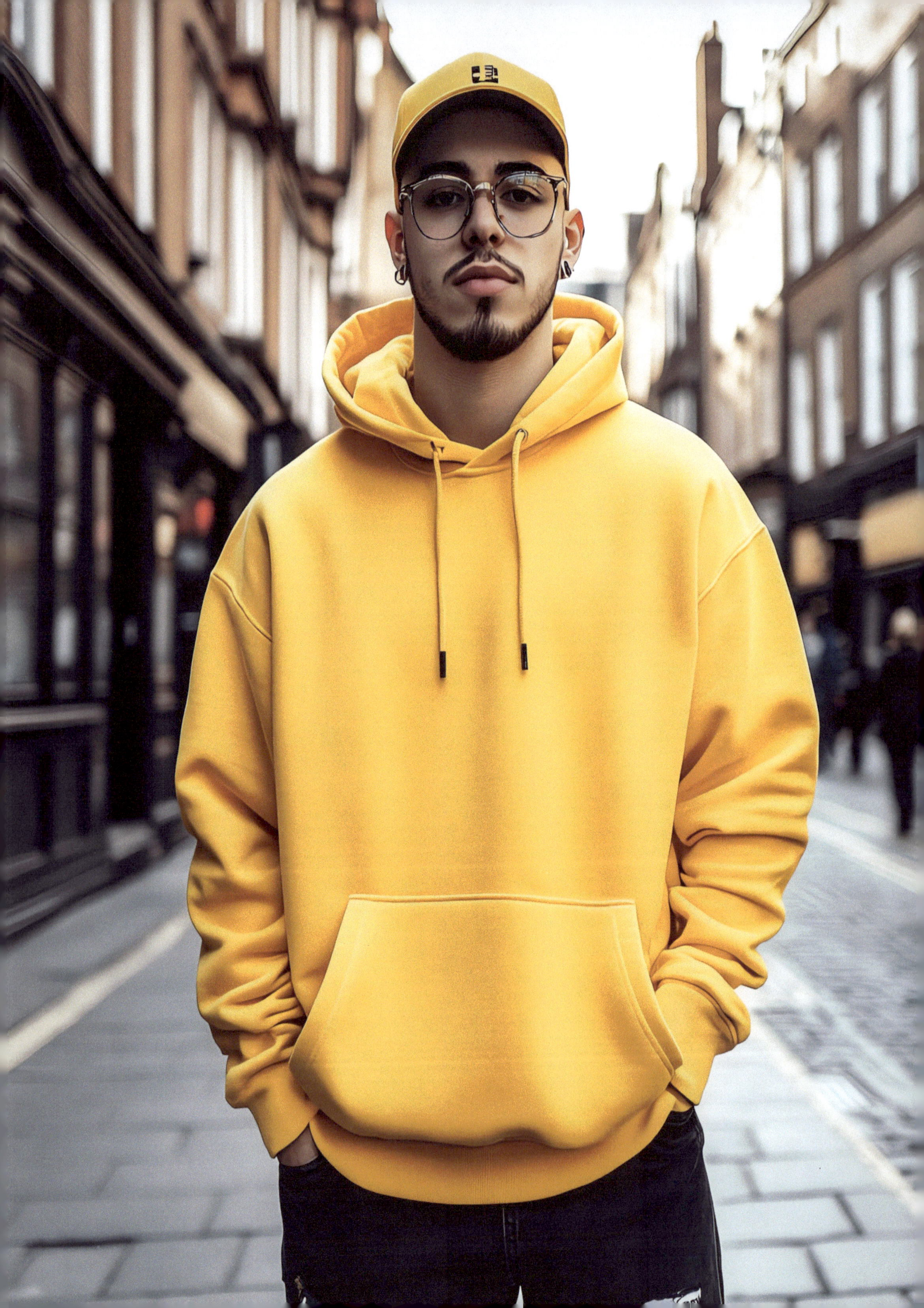

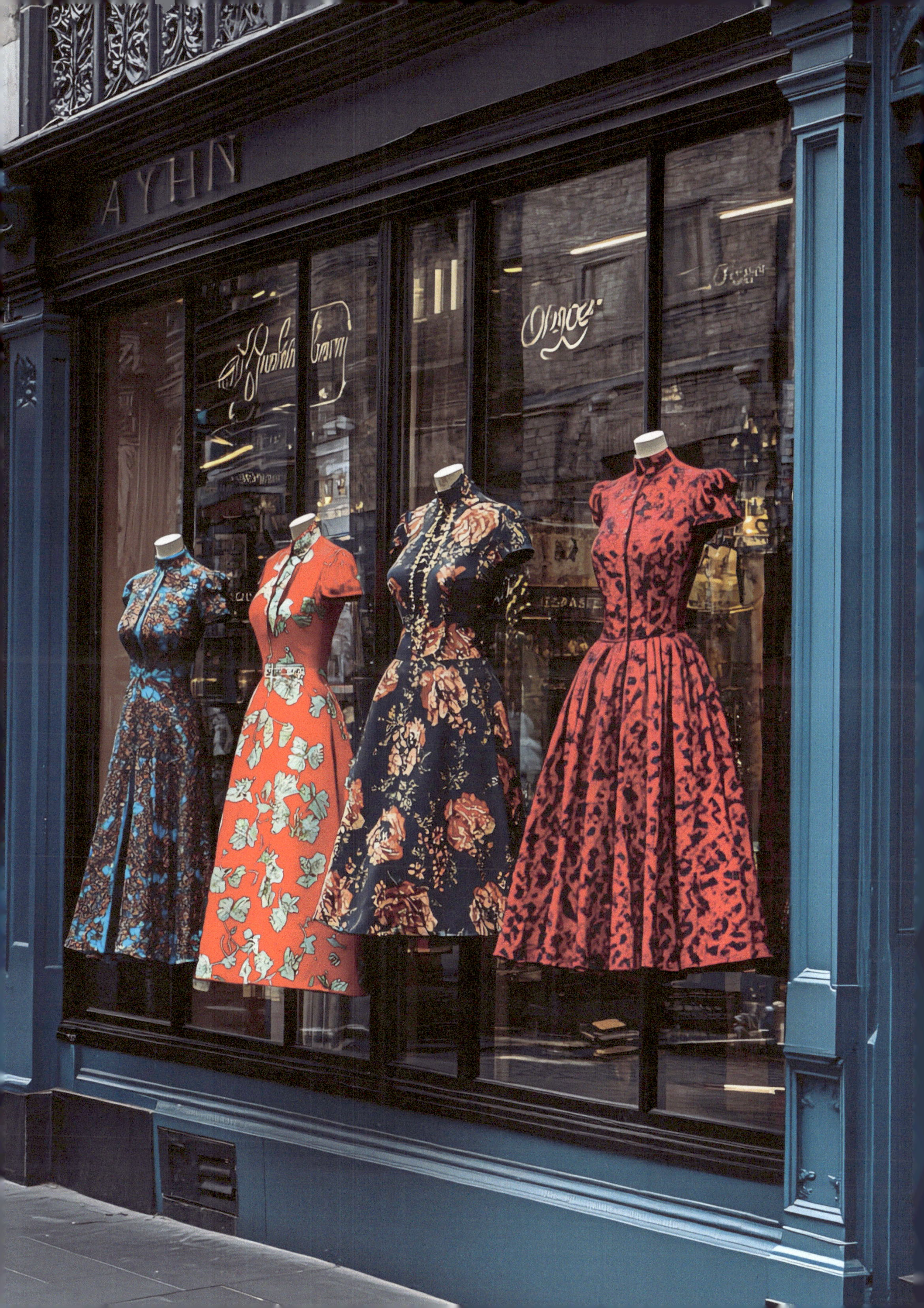

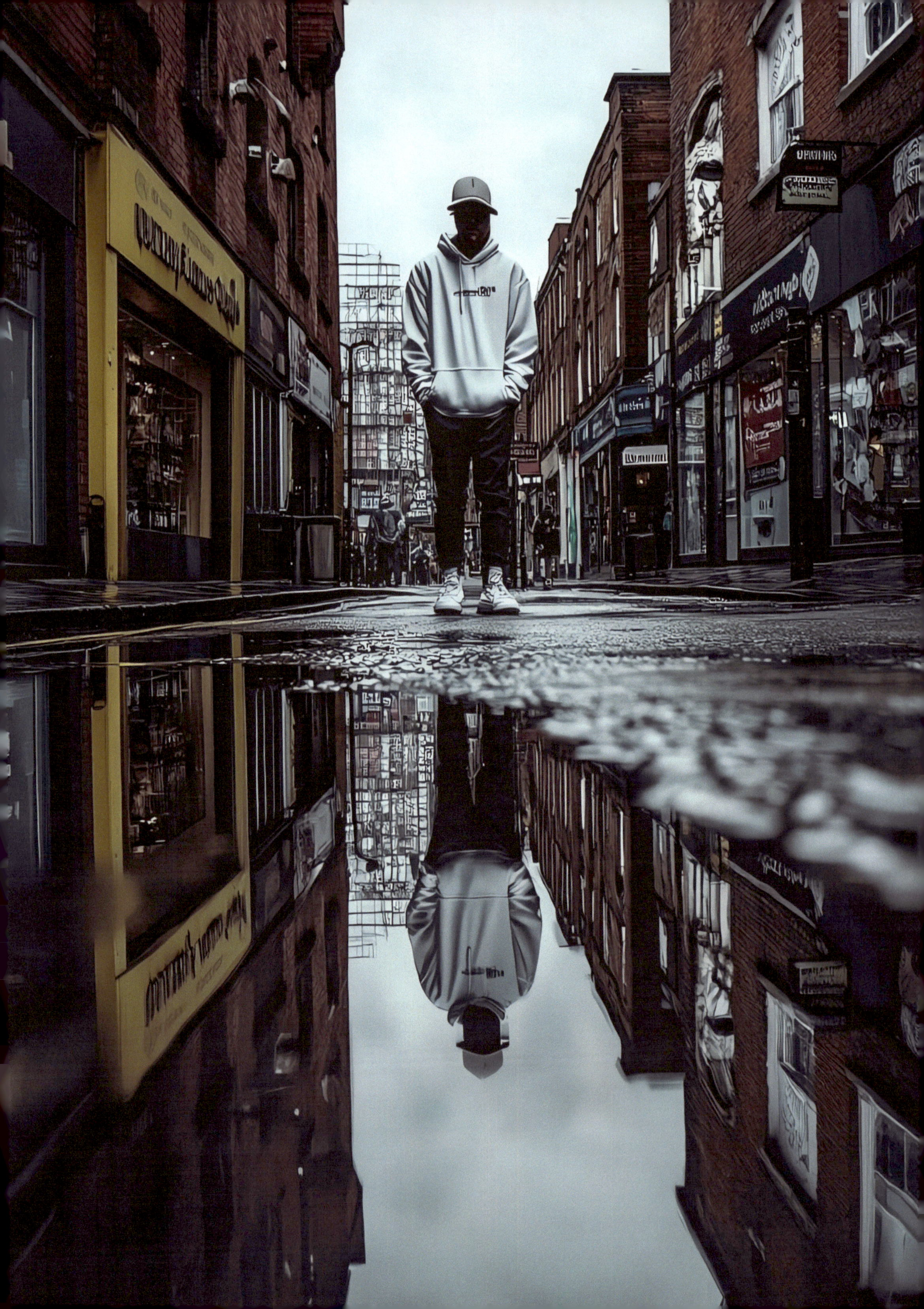

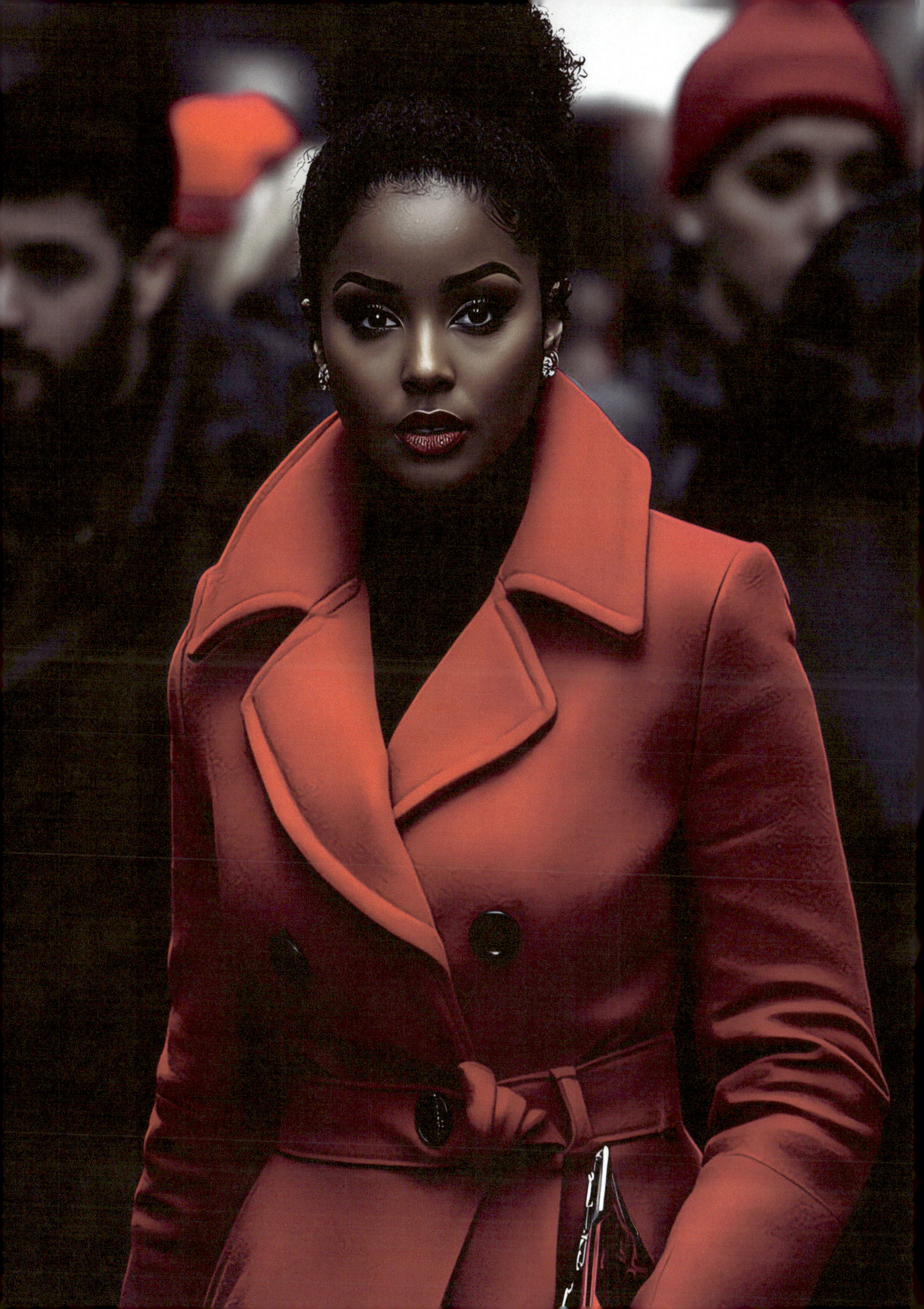

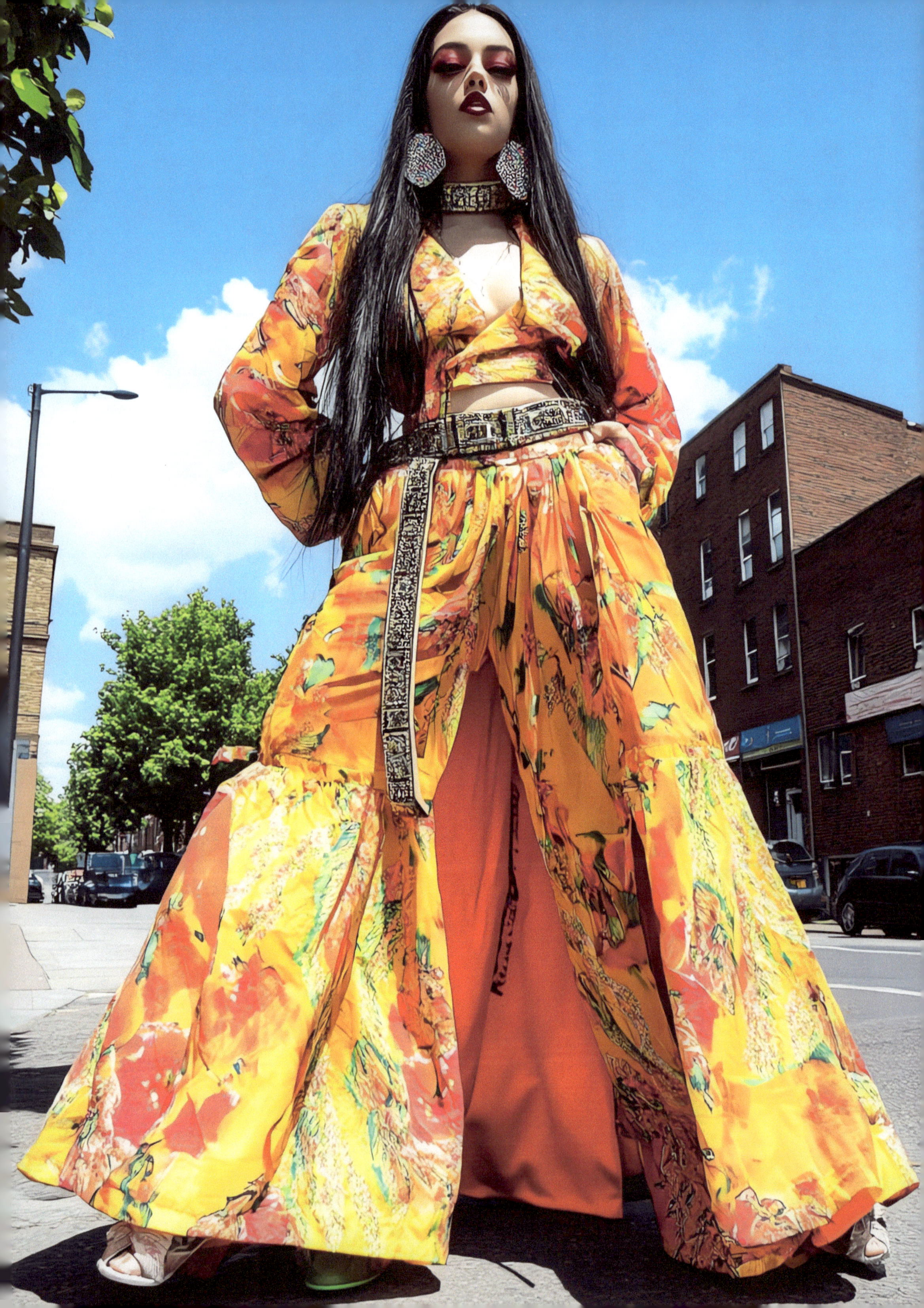

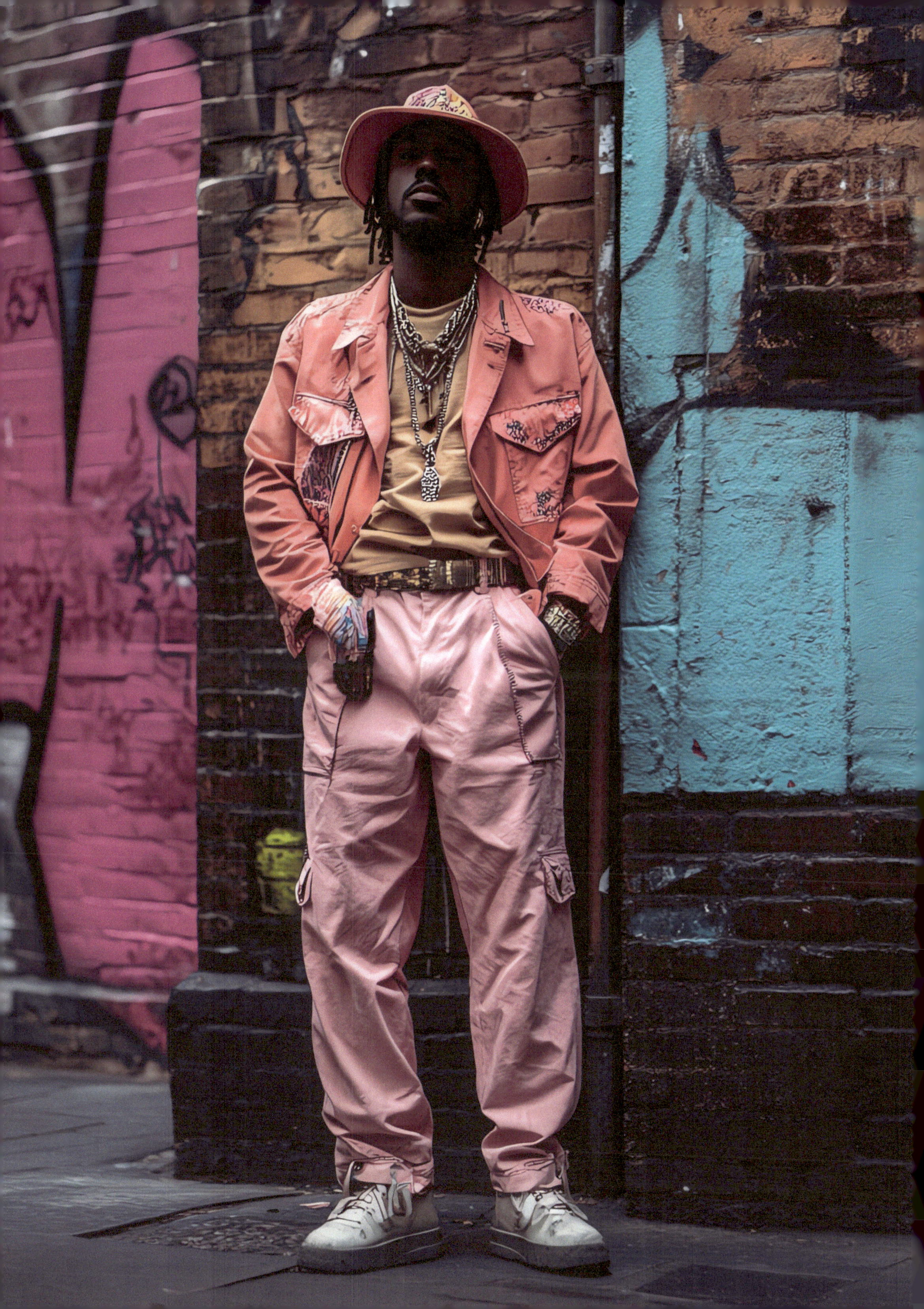

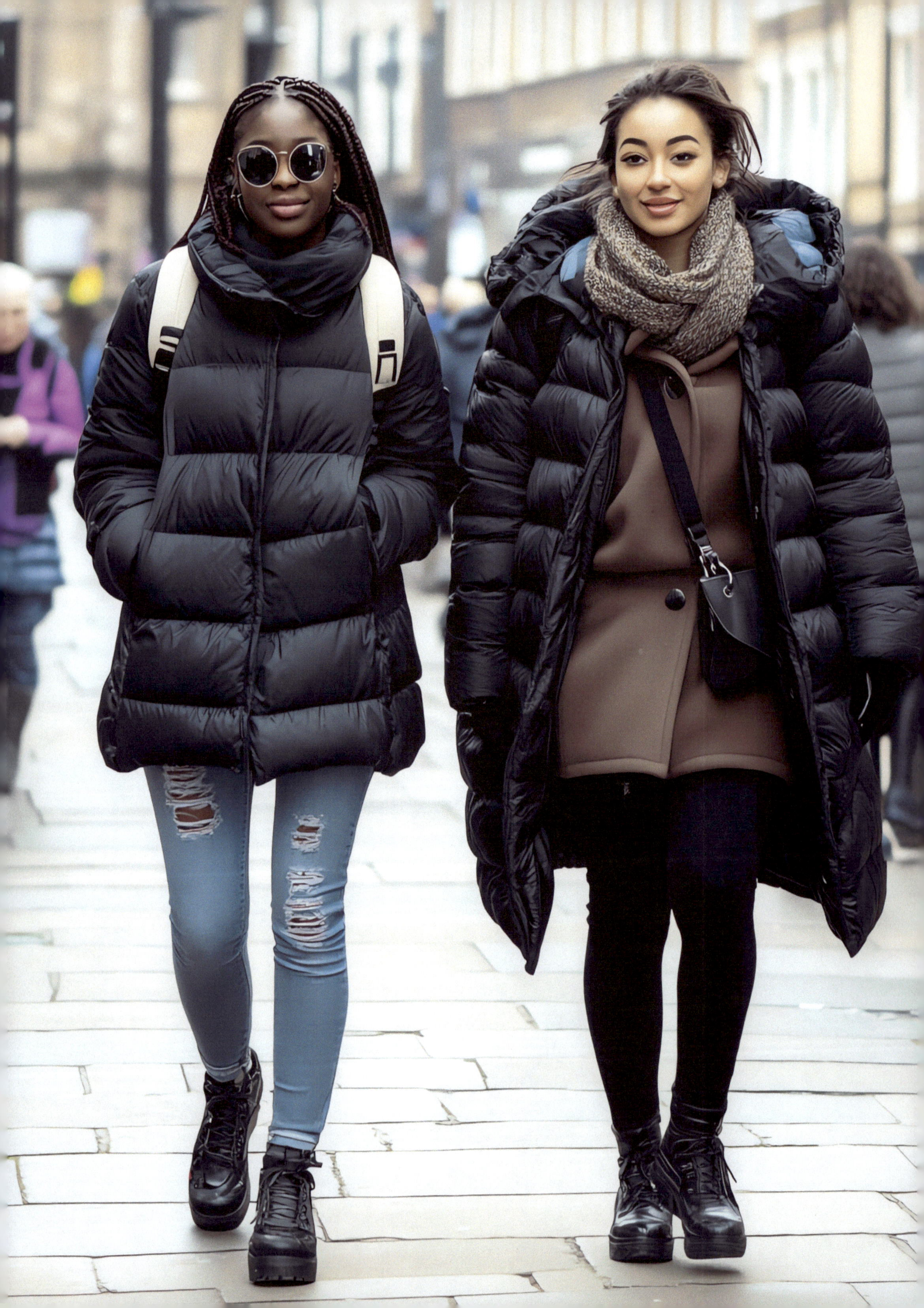

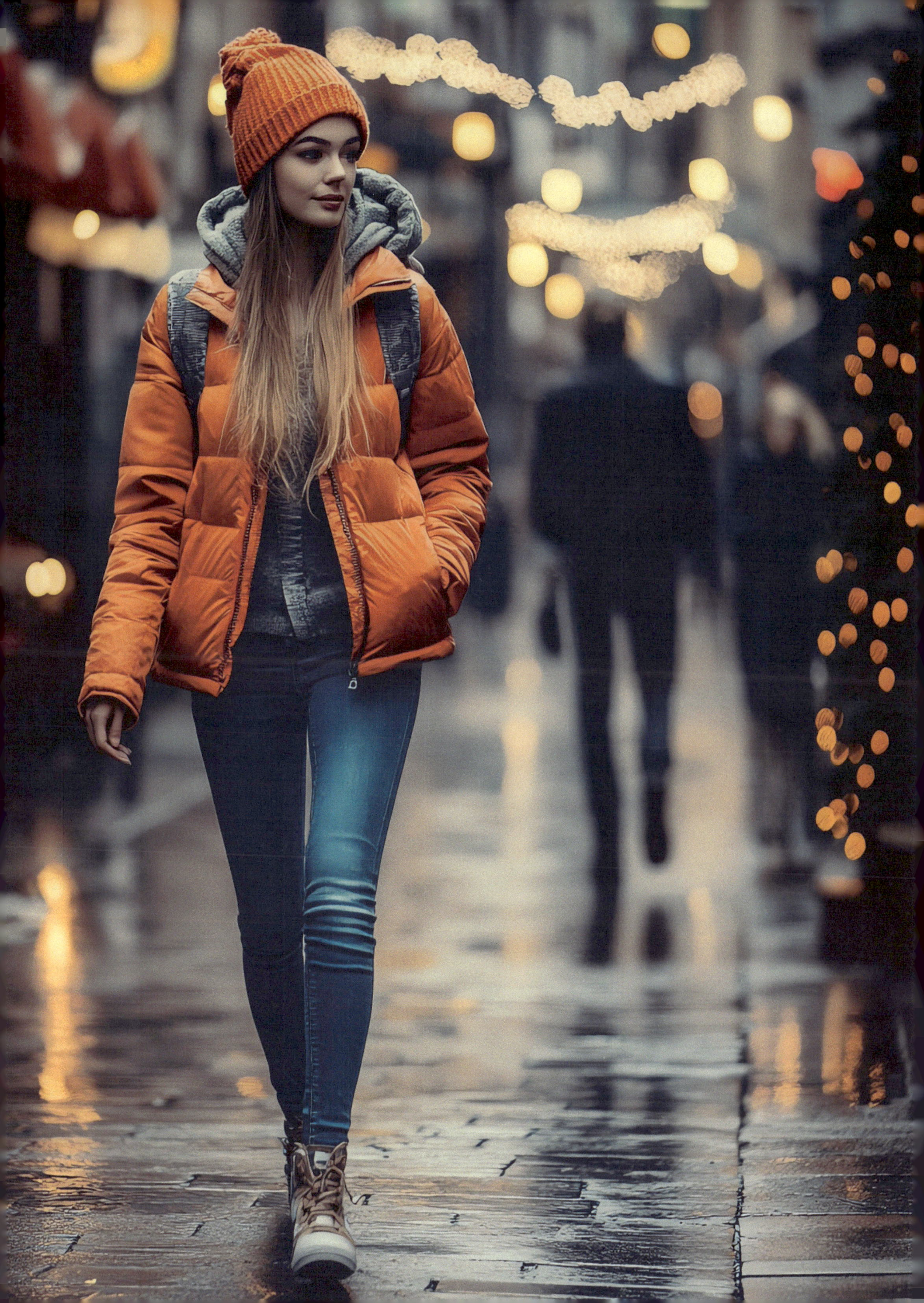

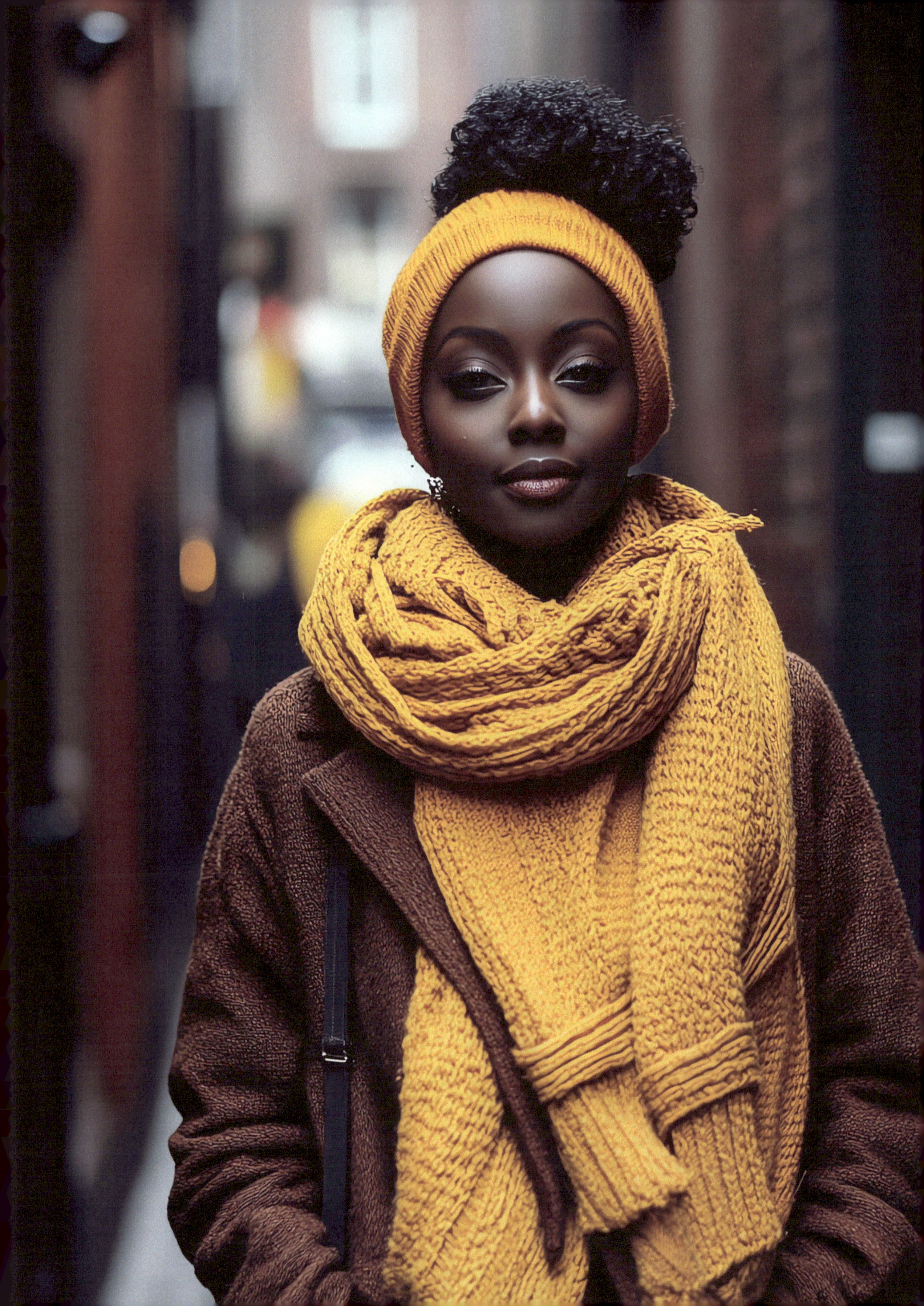

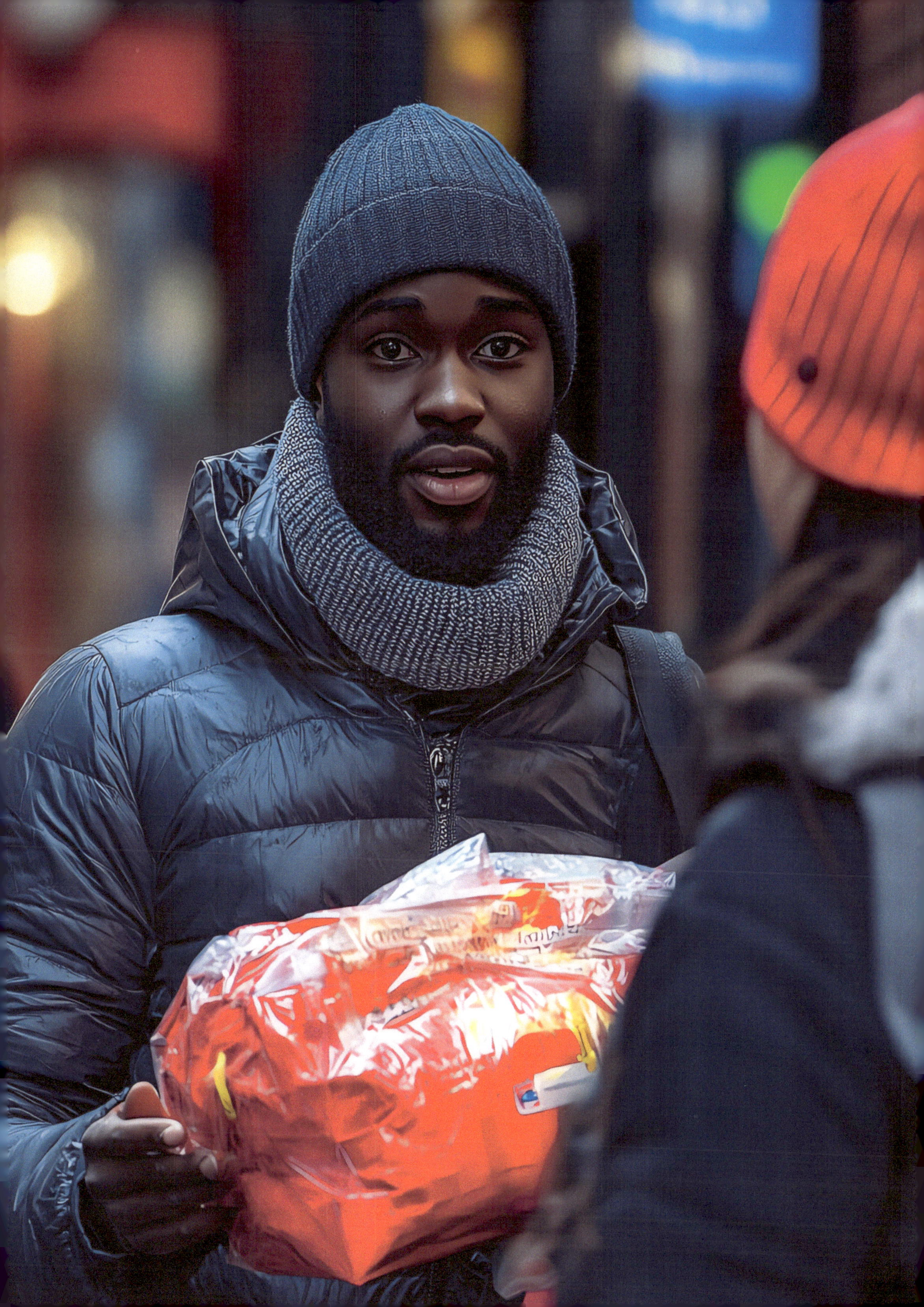

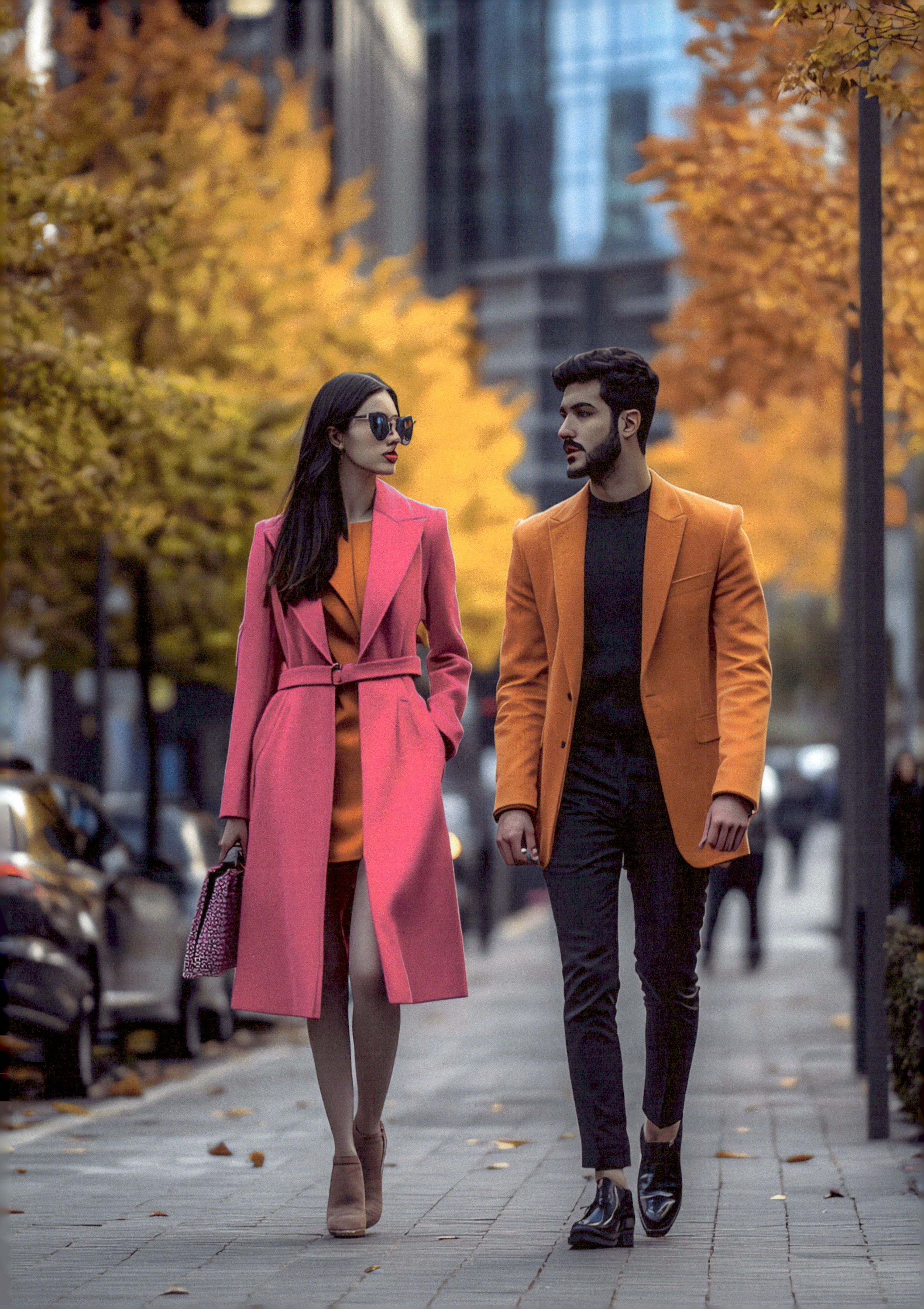

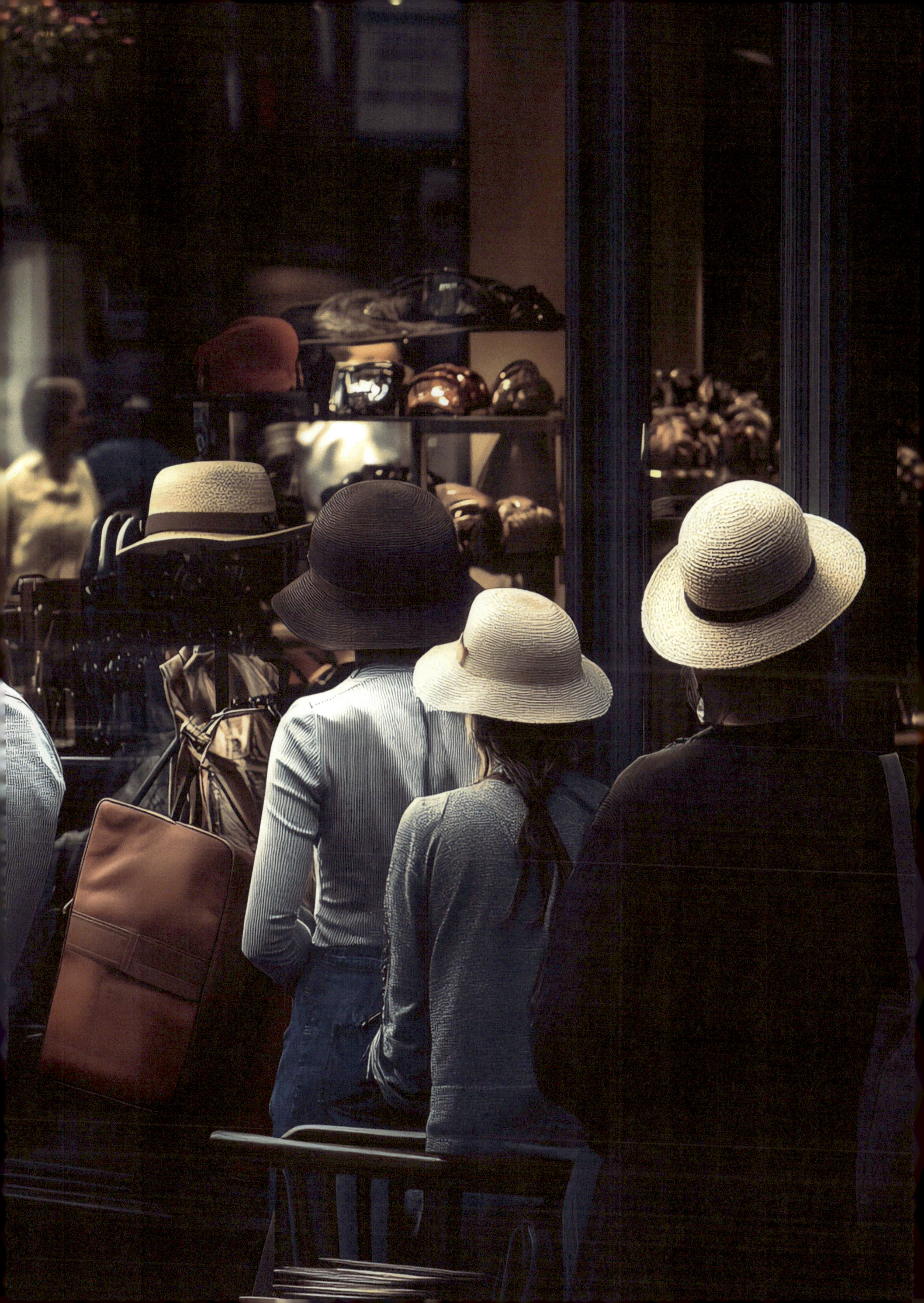

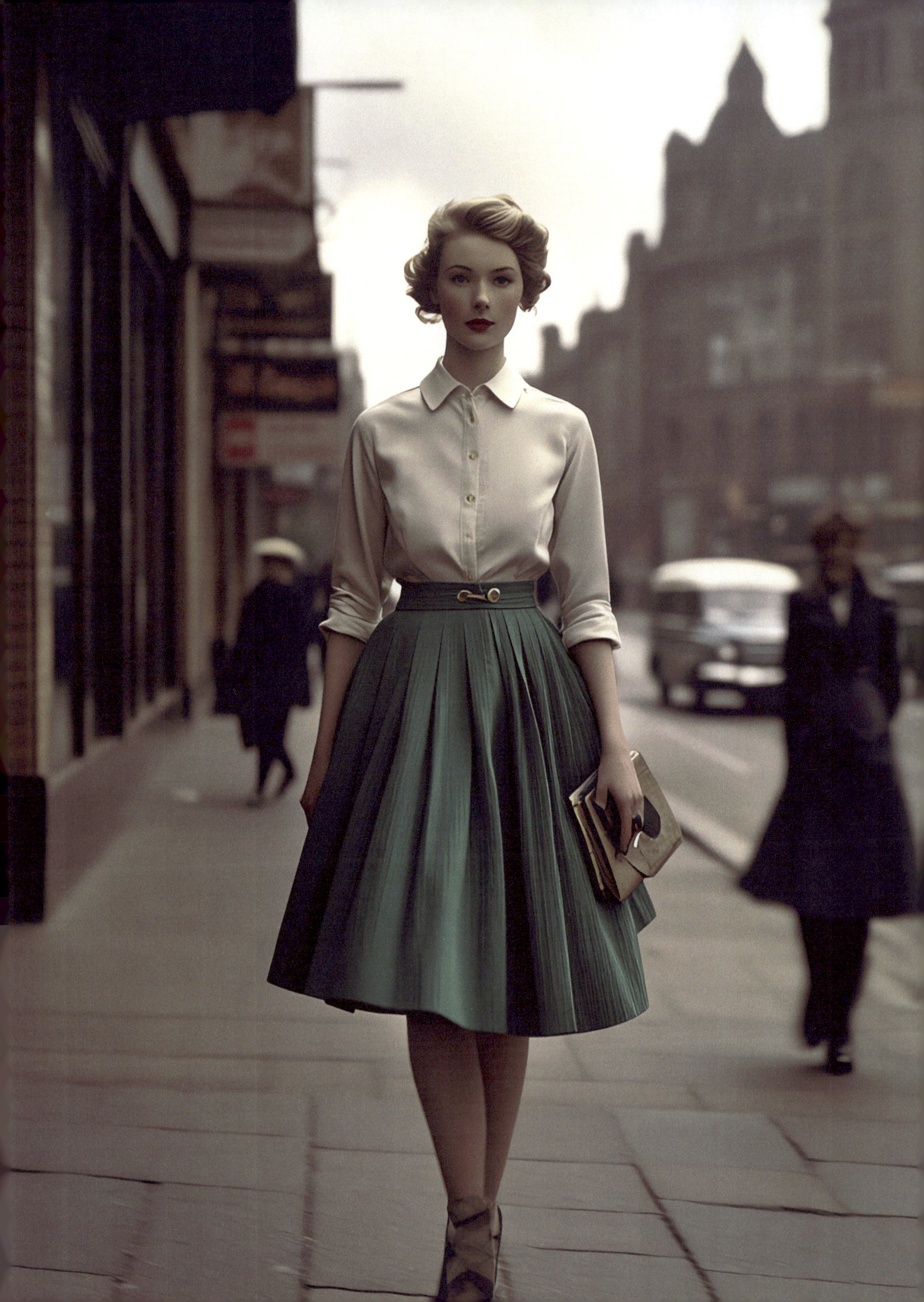

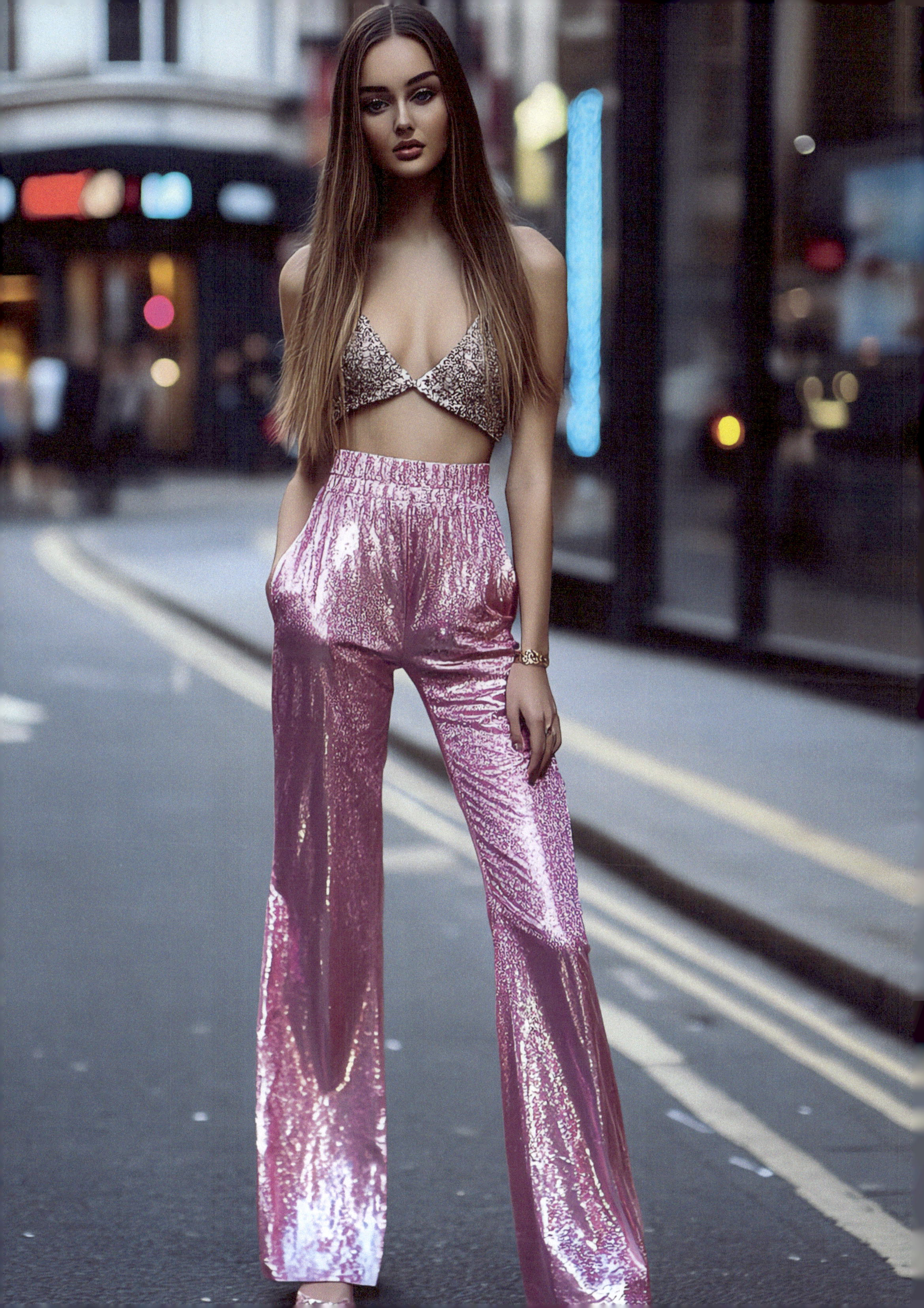

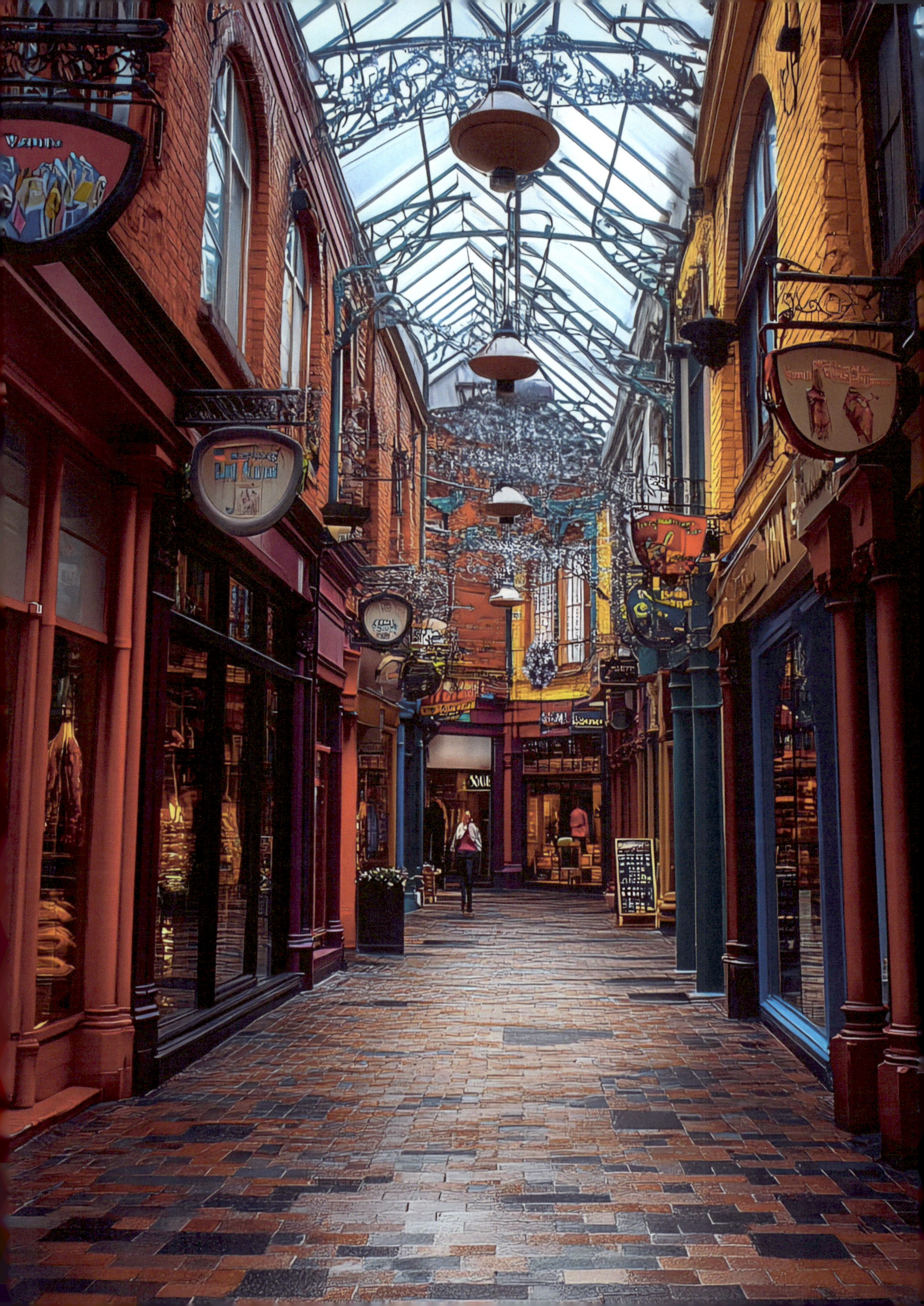

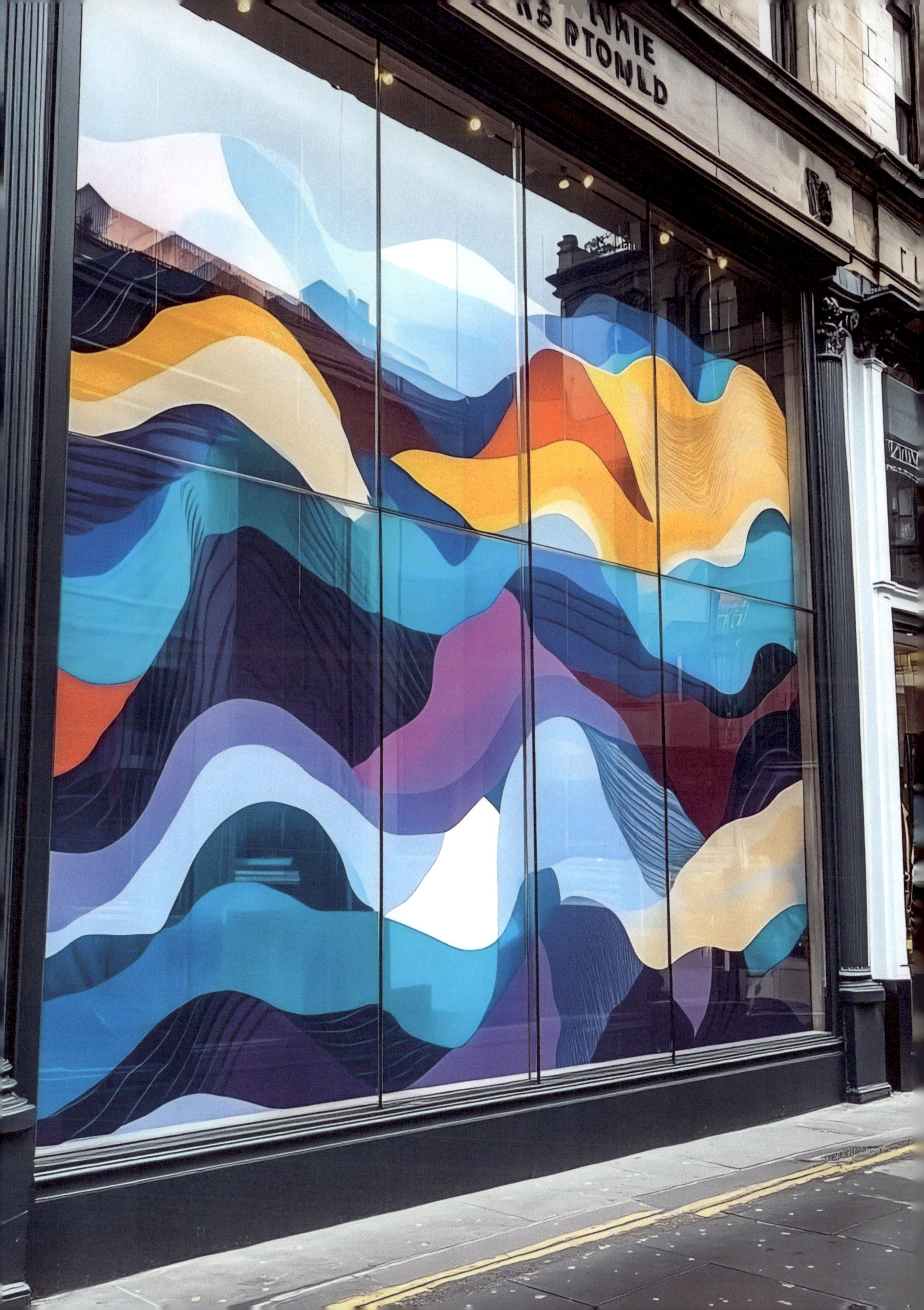

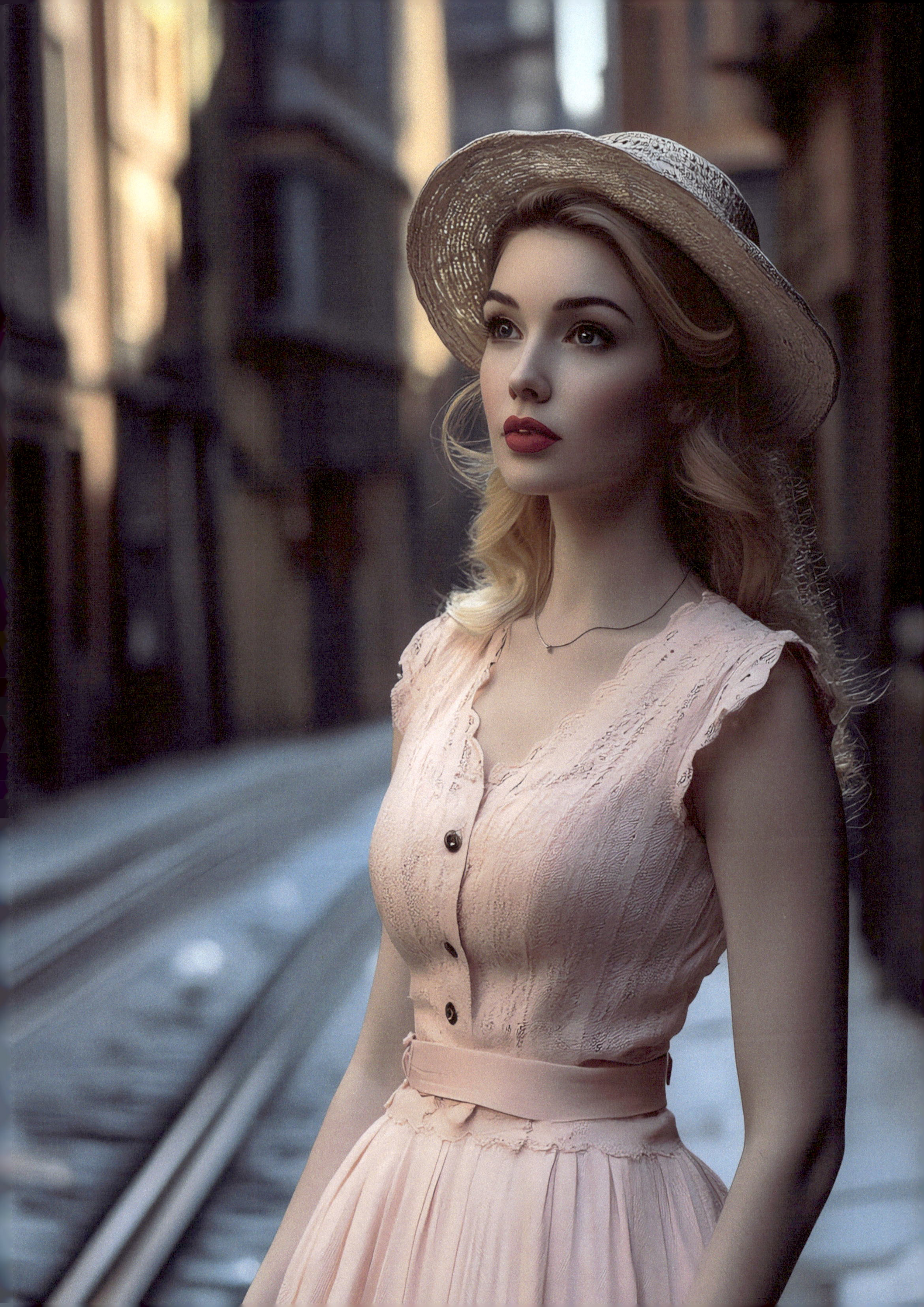

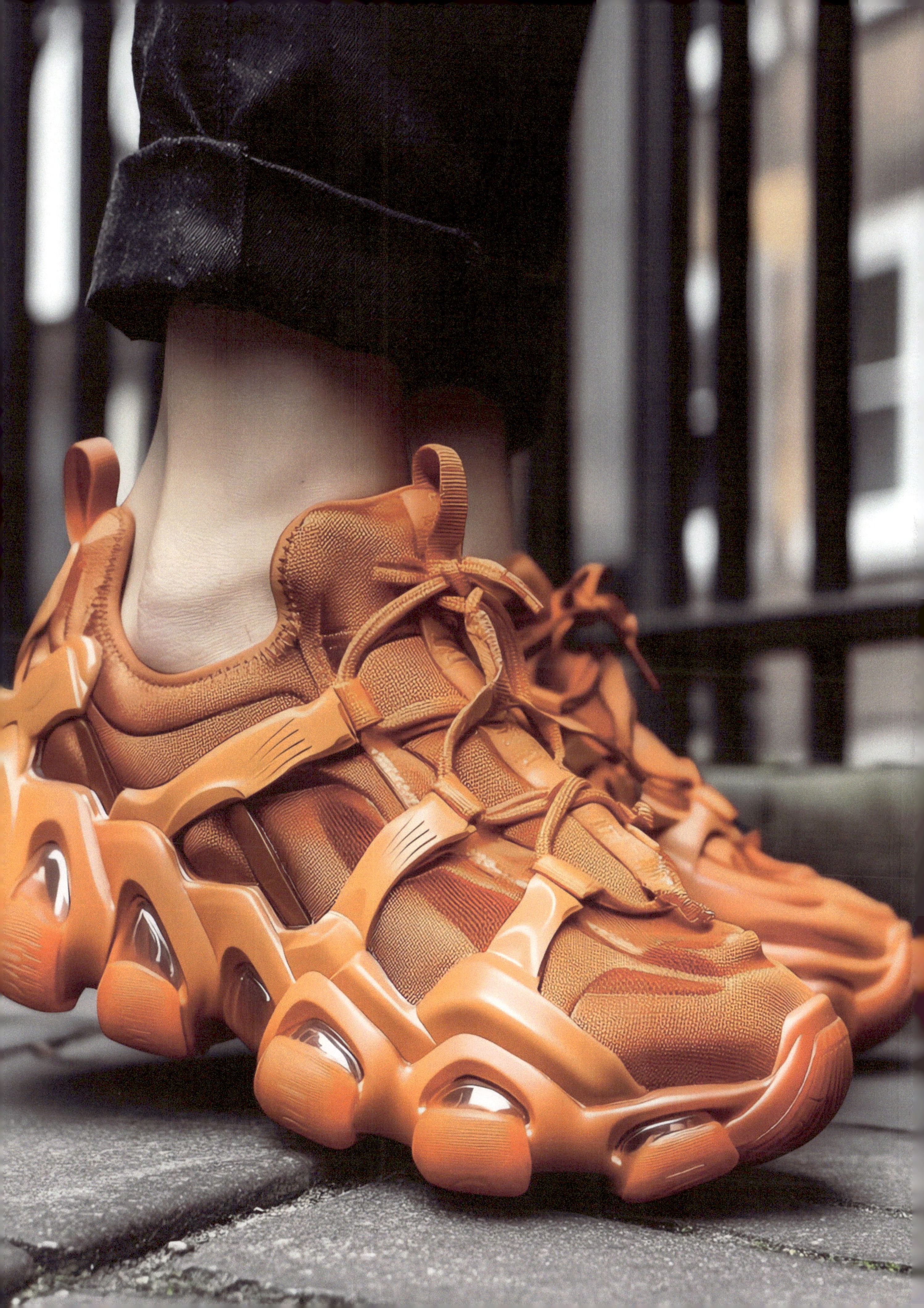

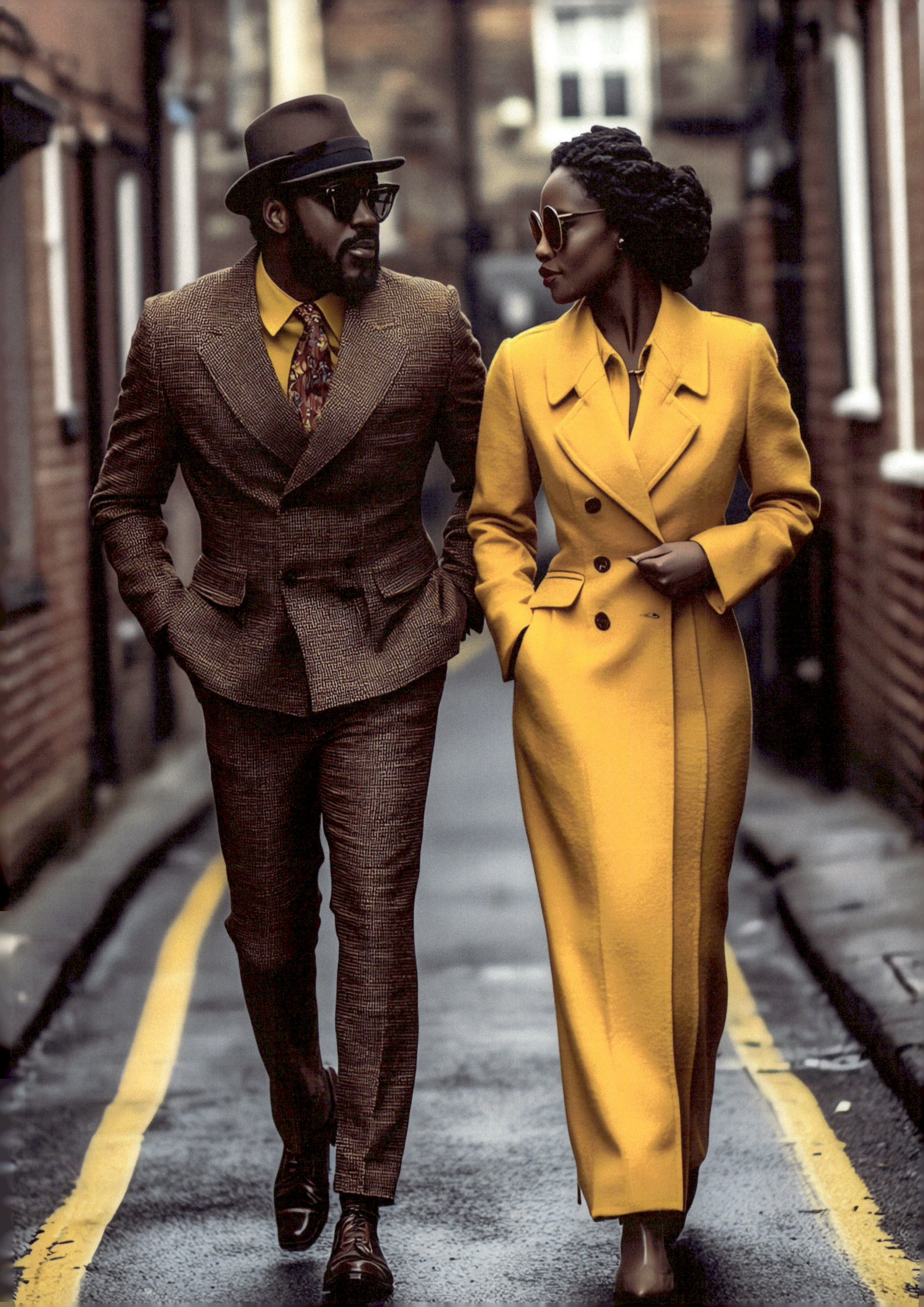